MAKE MONEY ONLINE AND INCREASE TRAFFIC

An Honest Book on Current Realistic Ways

Presented by Bruce Miller, B.A. J.D. And Team Golfwell

Published by Pacific Trust Holdings NZ Ltd.

Disclaimer:

This book discusses methods to earn passive income online, and to set up passive streams of income, and discusses active income online and ways to increase your traffic. It also discusses ways to set up passive streams of income you're your traffic increases. As with any business, your results may vary and will be based on your individual ability, business experience, ability, and level of desire. There are no guarantees concerning the level of success you may experience. Everyone's success depends on his or her background, dedication, desire and motivation.

This book is designed to give information on ways which earn online passive and active income and increase traffic. A lot of effort was made to make sure all information in this book is correct at the

About the Author

Bruce Miller is a former lawyer and former owner of two businesses who retired early after a demanding career. He found he needed something to keep active and became fascinated with ways to earn online income and increase traffic.

He is intrigued and passionate about how the internet is changing society and enjoys earning income online in many ways.

Bruce plays golf, has a lovely wife, and lives in New Zealand.

"Are you bored with your life?"

"Then throw yourself into some kind of work you believe in with all your heart, and live for it, and die for it."

"You will find a happiness that you thought could not ever be yours."

- Dale Carnegie

Contents

INTRODUCTION

There are no ads in this book – only income earning sites and ways to increase traffic for your blog, store or site.

This book is about online income and increasing traffic. Most of us need income. Section One of this book gives you ways to create passive income when you first start out when you don't have much traffic to your site or product.

Section Two gives you effective and realistic ways to increase traffic.

Section Three gives you more ways to earn passive income when you do have a lot of traffic.

Finally, Section Four gives you many ways to earn active income online.

If you want extremely straightforward and easy ways to earn income online, read the Mobile App Sub-section which can be found at the beginning of SECTION FOUR of this book.

With Mobile Apps (there are more than 15 apps explained in that subsection), you just download the app to your phone and begin

easily earning money right away. Jump ahead if you are interested to see what jobs are available on mobile apps which may appeal to you.

Years ago, when Team Golfwell first started, we spent a lot of time reading about how we had to buy a miracle guide, or take an amazing course, or attend an amazing seminar to make lots and lots of money online instantly. We got tired of reading sales hype telling us to buy their courses (some costing thousands), buy their book, pay a monthly subscription to learn how to earn on their site, and be filthy rich in no time, and retire on the beach for the rest of our lives.

Well I didn't like that, and being retired at an early age anyway, I had time on my hands to find reputable and knowledgeable sources. Besides, online income in intrigued us. We simply believe working hard at something you find enjoyable usually leads to success and a happy life.

We searched and searched for straight talk and realistic ways to earn online income and increase traffic and we want to share the sites and information which we found extremely helpful. We encourage more successful people to be honest and straightforward in sharing what works for them.

We believe reading this book makes it easier to learn about online income and increasing traffic since it clears you away from all the distractions on web pages. You can simply relax and read this book (and focus and learn) without anything else interfering your thoughts.

The internet and automation are causing many good people (who are competent at their job) to lose their job after years of faithfully working hard. For example, major retailers like Toys R Us and many other retailers are closing shop. Even though you may be quite good at your job, very few positions have indefinite employment (except perhaps a tenured university professor or a Supreme Court Justice).

It's especially important right now to set up sources (like passive income sources) that generate revenue for you and to allow the revenue to grow as the years go by. That will help you live a better life financially as your ability to earn income gradually fades with aging.

We feel most people believe having an excellent job they enjoy is one of the most important things in life as well as having as many streams of income established to increase their overall income.

If your goal is to be happy with your work and have established streams of online income, then you should read this book. It will make you aware of opportunities online right now and save you a lot of time and searching to get straight talk on these subjects.

When we first started we wished we had a straightforward (no bull) book like this to explain effective and current ways to earn online income and increase traffic. Now that we are earning steady online income, we decided to share what we found with other people, so they can find reliable information on realistic ways to earn income online, and ways to increase your traffic. Most of the ways discussed in this book do both.

We are not selling anything in this book to you and we do not earn any affiliate commissions or any type of referral income from any of the sites mentioned in this book.

A side note:

According to the American Psychological Association, humor produces psychological and physiological benefits that help people learn.

That is why we have mixed in the pages of this book several humorous stories which appear when you see the smiley face.

We find humor beneficial to learning and healthy. We hope you will learn a few new ways to earn income online and increase traffic and enjoy your learning.

Sit back and relax and see what methods of making money and increasing traffic interest you in this book.

"There is little success where there is little laughter."

- Andrew Carnegie

SECTION ONE: CREATING PASSIVE STREAMS OF ONLINE INCOME WHEN YOU <u>DON'T</u> HAVE TRAFFIC

There is a wide assortment of ways which we found exceptionally reliable to create large and small online income as well as reliable ways to increase your traffic. There is an 11-page Reference Section at the end of this book listing the sites we discuss in this book.

As you read through the pages, we want you to quietly review and evaluate these numerous sites without interference from the many distractions on the net, so you can determine what method(s) you might enjoy and be a good fit into your life.

Before describing ways to increase traffic, Section One describes ways to earn passive online income when you <u>don't</u> have a lot of traffic.

Passive online income means money earned when you aren't actively working, generates income when you're sleeping, recreating, or doing other things. You must spend some time in setting up the item or project that will generate passive income.

Examples of passive income streams where you don't need a huge amount of traffic are writing and self-publishing an eBook, selling your photos to Getty images, and many more. We will begin with eBooks.

E-Books and Print on Demand Paperbacks
Kindle Direct Publishing [1] & CreateSpace [2]

Dan Brown, Stephen King, John Grisham, are extraordinarily successful writers because people enjoy what they read in their books and continue to buy them (the content is the most important factor, i.e., "Content is king" [3]– there's much more about creating great content later in this book). Right now, the simple fact is if you can write a book that people enjoy reading, you will become better known and people will seek you out and buy and enjoy your writing.

For example, Amada Hocking writes mostly in the paranormal romance genre. Years ago, she needed a few hundred dollars (she was a huge fan of Jim Henson who was scheduled to be in Chicago, but she didn't even have enough money for gas to drive there).

So, she self-published one of her novels (which had been rejected by many conventional publishers) and she put her book for sale on Amazon. Two years later people who read her paranormal romance books simply enjoyed reading what she wrote. She sold 1.5 million copies of her books and she made over 2.5 million dollars and a New York Times Bestselling author.

If you enjoy writing, it's not hard to self-publish on Amazon companies like Kindle Direct Publishing[4] and CreateSpace.[5]

CreateSpace publishes your work in paperback and Kindle Direct Publishing will make your book available as an eBook or in paperback. Both will and distribute your paperback book on a Print on Demand basis (your book is printed when someone orders it).

KDP and CS help you create the book step by step as well as help you with the cover of the book, but the marketing of the book is solely up to you.

You don't have to write a 1,000-page novel. People write eBooks and Paperback books in every genre, short or long, fiction or non-fiction, reference books, journals, children's books, etc. and sell them on Amazon.

Books earn royalties for years without you having to do anything further. Royalties are shared 70% to you and 30% to Amazon (there are variations to this royalty split).

There is a lot of competition since there are millions of books for sale on Amazon. Some authors advertise their books using PPC advertising campaigns on Amazon via Amazon Marketing Services [6] creating ads getting their books out in front of Amazon shoppers.

If you advertise through Amazon Marketing Services, your book should begin to sell. Once it starts to sell and you get many honest reviews, Amazon itself will begin to promote the book. They do this by offering your book to customers who bought similar books, and other methods. In other words, Amazon promotes your book for free since

Amazon makes more money by promoting books that are selling. Once Amazon starts to promote it, you don't have to further advertise by PPC ads until your sales start to drop off, but hopefully, your book will become popular.

You should watch your Amazon Marketing Service ad campaigns once a day to make sure you are earning money. You do this by checking the "Advertising Cost of Sales" feature on the Campaign. When you do, you can tell at once if the cost of the ad is becoming non-profitable. Amazon explains the "Advertising Cost of Sales" or "ACoS" as the amount you've spent on a campaign divided by total sales during the campaign run dates. If you are on a 70% royalty, you don't want the ACoS to exceed 70% at any time.

Personally, our experience with Amazon thus far has been extremely good – our eBooks generate steady passive income monthly with little-added effort on our part. One thing to note though - Amazon pays 70% royalty on each eBook sold only if your eBook is priced between $2.99 to $9.99. Less than or higher than that pricing structure, the royalty decreases to 35% of your book's listed price.

You can also sell your book on other platforms like IngramSpark.[7] There is less competition on IngramSpark. You can contact retail stores to see if they have an interest in carrying your books. You can try to develop relationships with retailers, e.g. Airport Gift Stores, other retailers, etc. and generally market your book, arrange for book signings, etc. Amazon Author Central [8] will help you market as well.

IngramSpark [9] will also publish your book to book retailers. They will publish your book with a hardcover where Kindle Direct Publishing and CreateSpace do not offer hardcovers right now.

CreateSpace also has a dealer discount program to book retailers, or specialty shops, where retailers can buy copies of your paperback book at a discount from CreateSpace.

Getting your book on book retailer's shelves is difficult as book retailers reserve shelf space for books that sell. Hardly any book retailers will use their shelf space for books that don't sell. Besides, major publishers distribute large bookstores thousands of books on consignment for 90 days where small bookstores are ignored by large publishing houses and their distributors and small bookstores usually buy their books from wholesale suppliers like the Ingram Book Company and Baker & Taylor.

Most large bookstores order newly published titles directly from the titles' publishers/distributors. The retailer's margin is better for orders going through the publisher/distributor as opposed to going through wholesalers.

Marketing your book is up totally to you. There are many libraries, schools, and universities that buy books if your book meets their requirements. In your area (and wherever you want to sell your book), it might pay to research how those libraries, universities, etc. buy their books. A simple email from you enquiring will give you the answer. If they buy from suppliers, contact the suppliers, etc.

Most everyone wants a book that is selling and for it to sell, remember "Content is King" so concentrate on producing the best book you can, and people will spread the word, and retailers will seek out your book if it's selling.

Check the websites of Kindle Direct Publishing, CreateSpace and Ingram Spark to learn more about marketing your books. Avoid private blogs and websites (unless they are reputable, like

BookBub Partners [10] or Dave Chesson at Kindleprenuer [11] and have great references).

Amazon isn't the only place to sell books, although it's the most popular. There are other platforms to sell your book in eBook online like the Canadian site Kobo [12] or Apple iBook, [13] but Amazon presently dominates over the others.

If you are hard-pressed to find a niche to write about, it is always best to write about something you are familiar with and passionate about. There doesn't seem to be any limit on what people write about, e.g. "50 Things to Do with Your Grandchildren on Rainy Days", various "How to Books", Cook Books, Diet Books, Exercise Books, Biographies, etc.

If you enjoy writing, you should have a lot of fun doing books. Your goal is to write a book that people will tell their friends about it, and their friends will tell their friends, and so on.

You can publish your book on CreateSpace, Kindle Direct Publishing, IngramSpark and others if you own your own ISBN number. If you want an in-depth discussion on which platform to use, see this long article discussing Print On Demand and the differences between IngramSpark, CS and KDP.[14]

Keep in mind all these companies make constant changes in what they offer authors. So, it's always best to read a current article on what these companies are offering, and the costs involved if any.

You can have your book in an audiobook format using an Amazon-owned company called ACX.[15] You can narrate the book yourself, or partner with a professional narrator. You either pay the narrator a fee or negotiate with the narrator to see if he or she will do it for free and share in the future sales.

If you have made an app, Amazon sells apps internationally at its Amazon app store. [16]

Joe was a model husband. He worked long hours for a large publishing firm working for a promotion. He was overly ambitious and a model husband.

Trying to stay fit, Joe religiously went to the gym two nights a week, and he played golf every Saturday.

His wife of two years was happy he was such a determined man, but she wanted him to relax more.

She decided to surprise him and take for his birthday to a local Gentleman's Club one evening.

When they drove up, the parking valet at the Club opened the door for Joe's wife. He then went around and took the keys from Joe.

"Nice to see you again, Joe." The parking valet said.

His wife wondered, "Joe, have you been here before?"

"No, haven't ever been here. That guy goes to the same gym I do."

They get a table up front and the server brings Joe a bourbon and water. "Here's your usual Joe, what would your guest like to drink?"

Joe's wife orders a wine, then says, "How'd she know you like bourbon and water?"

"She's a bartender at the golf course and knows that's what I drink, sweetheart."

A dancer comes up to their table and musses Joe's hair with both her hands and says, "Hi Joey-Joey, you want your usual lap dance tonight?"

Joe's wife is fuming and grabs her purse and storms out the door. She waves a taxi down outside. Joe follows her and just gets into the taxi before his wife can slam the door on him. Joe begins pleading with his wife explaining the dancer must have mistaken him for someone else. He begs her to understand.

Joe's wife is going bezerk, yelling at him non-stop. She's using every four-letter expletive known to man. Joe continues pleading when the taxi driver turns around and says, "You picked up a real bitch this time, Joe."

Lending Club [17]

Making a loan and receiving repayments is passive income as to the interest part of the repayment. There are several opportunities for you to become a lender through online lending sites.

If you are looking for a higher return than what banks pay, making a loan and getting repaid at a higher interest rate than what most banks pay might be beneficial.

The <u>Lending Club</u> [18] is a site where you can invest money to be loaned out to others and it works like this:

I'll start with an example. A lot of people borrow money to consolidate high-interest credit card debt to a lower interest rate by getting a loan at a lower interest rate and pay off high-interest credit card debt. They then have one payment at a lower interest rate which will save them money in the long run.

People can apply for a loan through the Lending Club site. They fill out an application online with the Lending Club. The Lending Club reviews their application and assesses the risk, investigates, and determines the applicant's credit rating. The Lending Club then assigns an appropriate interest rate. If the interest rate is lower than what the applicant is paying for credit cards, the person will usually take the loan from the Lending Club.

If you decide to invest some of your funds via the Lending Club site, you first join the Lending Club as an <u>Investor</u>.[19] As an Investor, you review the Lending Club site for various (and numerous) lending opportunities the Lending Club displays. You decide whether or not to invest your funds for a particular loan. The investors who use Lending Club range from institutions to average individuals.

After the loan is made to the applicant, each investor receives monthly payments of principal and interest until the loan is paid off.

The entire process is online, using technology to lower the cost of credit and to pass the savings back in the form of lower rates for borrowers. Investors usually enjoy a better return than what most banks pay.

Caution: There is *always* a risk any loan will go delinquent and uncollectable due to unforeseeable events. So, you don't want to invest money you need or may need in the future. You should only invest money you can afford to lose. Also, keep in mind the adage, "The higher the risk, the higher the reward," as interest on bank accounts or a bank time deposit, involves an exceptionally low risk.

Also, to reduce the risk of one Lending Club loan going bad and uncollectible, you can invest say $5,000 (for example, or some other amount of money that you could afford to lose) and divide it up into $25 investments in 200 different loans to spread your risk.

Fundrise [20]

Another online investment site is Fundrise. This was the first site to successfully crowdfund investment into the real estate market.

Instead of investing into a pool of money to loan out to borrowers who make an application for a loan like the Lending Club, you can invest a small amount of money into Real Estate Investment Trusts commonly referred to as REITs.

Your investment goes into a fund with funds from others to buy real estate and you own a share and become part of the REIT. There are fees, ongoing reports, etc. see the Fundrise FAQs. [21]

Sell Your Photos

There are many sites on the web where you can sell your photos and receive royalty payments generated by people who buy your photos.

Here are some well-known photo buying sites:

Getty Images,[22] iStockphotos,[23] Foap,[24] Shutterstock [25]

These sites (there are many more) buy photographs. Getty Images is the largest. Many people need photos for book covers, articles, display material, etc. and buy photos from these sites at a reasonable cost.

Companies like Shutterstock and iStockphotos pay you each time one of your photos is downloaded by a customer. If you sold one of these sites your amazing photo(s), it could be downloaded several times per day and you earn a small percentage of each sale and this can add up.

Foap also has a feature on their site called "Foap Missions" [26] where businesses pay $100 or more per photo if they chose your photos for the specific "Mission". On Foap, businesses post a description of what they are looking for (i.e., the "Foap Mission") and what they will pay, all listed on the Foap site.

The mission is described very well – you can view examples of the various missions by visiting Foap homepage and you will see a drop-down menu under "Brands". Click on "Foap Missions" [27]to view a sample mission.

Snapwire [28]

Snapwire is a platform that connects businesses with photographers and videographers. Photographers are referred to as "Creators" and as a Creator, you can sell photos to businesses who are looking for certain images.

Businesses or other people post on Snapwire what they want, and photographers submit and sell their photos to them. The businesses describe what their requirements are and what kind of photos or videos they need to fulfill those requirements. This is called a Request. Photographers submit their photos through Snapwire and the business decides whether or not they fulfill the Request and if so, the photographer is paid.

Businesses want real-world photos, as the posed and staged photos don't get as much attention anymore.

Snapwire is a site where smartphones make it easy to catch action photos that businesses want those photos more than conventional posed photos.

Taking great real-life photos with your smartphone also applies to boosting your Instagram photos and videos as well.

See the two photos below, the first is a male model posing (the faraway look has become too common and inundating the web). The second photo is a real-world photo of a happy couple approaching you with a smile and conveying a message to the viewer (along with a warm feeling) that being fit is great and they are enjoying themselves golfing and are happy to see you.

You may not know everything a professional photographer knows, but keep in mind developing a photographic eye is more important than knowing how to run the most complex camera.

There are many high-quality books/videos available to teach you basic digital photography like "Tony Northrup's DSLR Book: How to Create Stunning Digital Photography," [29] which has been a bestseller.

In regard to developing a photographic eye, have you ever been on a photography class field trip where 20 students wander around a farm or wooded area and take photographs? Even though everyone takes photos in the same place, only one or two students produce amazing photos due to their artistic eye is seeing and framing the shots?

Being able to take great photos is especially important in today's world. Here is a step by step approach on how to develop a photographic eye.

- o Wander around with your camera looking at various places and without bringing your camera up to your eye, picture and frame the subject you want to photograph first before looking at it through the camera. Train yourself to see the shot first before you use the camera.

- o Once you have the picture you want in your mind, raise the camera and try to recreate it with the camera.

- o Imagine different lighting effects on your subject. Think about what light will enhance the subject more and decide on it and a time of day the light you want will most likely appear.

- o If you have difficulty forming a picture from the area you are in, take a picture of the entire area. Then look at the big picture and study it and select a portion of the big picture that looks interesting and would capture people's attention.

- o Go into your kitchen and place one ordinary object on the counter (such as a stainless-steel pot or skillet, or a can of soup) and walk around the object studying how the light hits it. Look at the object up close and at a distance. Decide on what you want your photo of this object to look like before you look through the camera at it.

- o Close your eyes and imagine a beautiful scene or something unusual and exciting that would catch people's interest. Then try and recreate the scene in real life.

Over time, you can develop an artistic eye especially when you see which of your photos sell more than others.

*

Joe got divorced from his wife, met another woman and decided to get married again. He proposed, and she accepted, and they planned a large beautiful wedding.

Joe paid everything for an extravagant wedding ceremony. They were being married in a huge Church.

As the soft-spoken minister began the marriage ceremony, the Church became silent. The minister routinely asked if anyone in the church had anything to say or a reason the two should not get married, "Speak now, or forever hold your peace," the minister said.

There was a quick moment of utter silence which was broken like a bolt of lightning when a gorgeous young woman carrying a newborn baby stood up in the last pew and started walking toward the minister slowly.

The newborn's cries and whimpers echoed as the young girl continued to approach the front of the church. All eyes instantly focused on her.

Chaos ensued quickly. The bride threw her flowers in Joe's face. The groomsmen winked at each other, and the wide-eyed bridesmaids couldn't believe what they were seeing.

The bride's father got up and took a wild swing at Joe, then put his arm around his daughter, and took her out of the church.

Joe couldn't believe what was happening but stood his ground as the young woman and newborn approached him and the minister.

Most of the wedding guests got up and began to head for the exits.

The minister asked the woman, "My dear woman, why on earth did you come up here? What is your reason?"

The young woman replied, "We can't hear anything way in the back of the church."

Create Your Own App

Just like many people started building their own website in the initial stages of the internet, it's easier now to build your own app than it was years ago.

On the downside, there is a lot of competition among apps and a little over 10% of all apps get more than 50,000 downloads. You also must compete against professional app developers who may spend thousands marketing new apps.

An example of an extraordinarily successful app built by people with no prior app building experience is "Koi Pond" (build your own fishpond).

If you are going to build an app, it's good to have a basic understanding of Java, the most widely used programming language. There are also programs you will need to download such as SDX, Eclipse, and more which will help you build an app for Androids.

There are sites which will help you build an app such as, AppyPie,[30] or AppMakr,[31] and there are others as well.

If you have a good idea for an app but find it hard to use AppyPie or other app building sites, you can hire others to do an app for you through Upwork [32] or Fiverr [33] and other sources. You must be careful in selecting who will do the work for you. It's best to consider using a service you find on Upwork or Fiverr only after you read all the reviews and compare the service with other services. You might want to also contact the person you want to build the app for you for more information and look at his past work to see the quality of his work.

If you have an original idea for an app, you need to protect your idea and in the very least, have the contractor who will build the app for you, sign a confidentiality agreement before you discuss the app in detail with him. Seek legal advice if you have any doubts or questions about this. And, communicate with the person who is going to do the work to make sure you and he knows what you expect, and he has the skill to build your app.

Once you have your app completed either by yourself or by a service, you then must market and sell it, so it will generate future passive income. Some app developers offer new apps for free with add-on paid options. There is Amazon marketing advice [34] offered on the Amazon App Store.

Udemy [35]

If you are an academic or have special expertise in an area you think people would enjoy learning, Udemy is the largest marketplace in the world where people buy courses to learn something.

You can create a course and market it to millions of people shopping on Udemy for courses. You create the course and then earn passive income from future sales.

There are many courses on Udemy and it's extremely competitive. High-quality courses sell over most others. This means you need a good deal of technical ability and it may be expensive to create the course. If you have a unique and original idea for a course, research Udemy to see what your competition might be.

A lot of courses use video and sites like Vimeo [36] to create the video. Vimeo is a large and popular platform to help you create videos for your course.

Skillshare [37]

Skillshare is another platform where you can create courses for free and Skillshare takes a percentage fee when people enroll to take your course.

There are thousands of courses on Skillshare on most any subject you can think of such as photography, high tech, design, business, entrepreneurship, writing, etc. If you believe you have a unique and popular idea for a course that will solve people's problems or enhance their lives, research and see if there are similar and competitive courses on Skillshare as well as Udemy. Keep in mind your idea may be what a lot of people are looking for.

*

After the fiasco at the church, Joe's fiancé understood that wasn't Joe's baby and they later got married. Joe loved his new bride very much, but when they returned from their honeymoon, they weren't talking to each other. Not one bit.

Joe went to work the next day and his boss asked him, "Hi Joe, how the honeymoon go?"

"Okay at first, but I was single for a while after my divorce and I wasn't getting used to married life just yet."

"What do you mean 'Not used to it," his boss asked?

"After we finished having sex, I put a $100 bill on the pillow – it was just habit and I didn't think twice about it."

"Wow! You are in trouble, Joe! Maybe your wife will feel better with time?"

"Hell, I'm not concerned about her. The problem I have is she left $80 change!"

Airbnb [38]

Through Airbnb, you can start your own "Bed and Breakfast" where you rent out spare rooms, apartments, homes, holiday homes, even house trailers, etc.

Airbnb is both passive and active income. Passive income is the rental you receive, and active income is you actively working to check them in and supply a breakfast for your guests. Check with your tax advisor to be sure and for how Airbnb income will affect your taxes.

Airbnb charges a small commission for each booking. Travelers search the site and view maps with available places they can stay at and travelers usually pick a convenient place for themselves. Airbnb prices are much lower than hotels.

But on Airbnb, all types of properties are available at varying prices. Rentals can be modest or extravagant. Owners can require a two-day minimum stay of guests through Airbnb, a week, or more.

Turning a room in your home can generate a lot of passive income. There is a straightforward and simple checklist of things to do to turn a room into a guest room at the end of this Airbnb explanation for you.

You can approve or disapprove guests who contact you to stay at your home.

To set up on Airbnb, take good photos and describe all the features of what you are renting out and explain other conveniences in your area which travelers might like such as good restaurants, transportation, etc.

Guest pay in advance through Airbnb. You can set your own cancellation policy, e.g. no refunds within 24 hours of arrival, etc.

Join Airbnb and see what property owners are offering in your area, the rates they charge, the policies on reservations, etc. to give yourself an idea of whether this would be financially beneficial to you.

You can request damage deposits and charge the guest for breaking or damaging things in your home through Airbnb. Airbnb also offers insurance for guest damage and other matters. Contact Airbnb customer service (in the US their telephone is: 1-415-800-5959 or check for other contact numbers in your area if you have questions).

Sample Airbnb Checklist for a Guest Room

Bathroom:

- Bath Towels
- Beach Towels (if relevant)
- Towel Hooks
- Toilet Paper (plan for about 1.5 rolls per week)
- Feminine Products
- Hair Dryer
- Magnified Makeup Mirror
- Shower Hanger (for toiletries)

Suggestions for Toiletries

- Hand Soap

- o Shampoo
- o Conditioner
- o Body Wash
- o Combs
- o Toothpaste
- o Disposable Toothbrush
- o Disposable Razors
- o Body Lotion

Sleep area:

- o Bed Linens and Pillows (for laundering & restocking linen services, click here)
- o Extra Linens, Blankets, and Pillows
- o Air Con, Heater, and/or Fan
- o Garbage Bin
- o A Box of Tissues
- o Pen & Note Pad
- o Bedside Table
- o Bedside Lamp
- o Foot Rug
- o Alarm Clock
- o Dresser and/or Shelves (at least one unit)
- o Safe for Passports and Valuables

If there is a lounge area:

- o Books and Magazines
- o Desk or Workspace

- o Coloring Books and Crayons
- o Pens and Pencils
- o Playing Cards

Make sure you follow all local and state regulations concerning smoke detectors, fire extinguishers, first aid kits, emergency numbers,

You can add or take away as much as you like. The more you provide to your guests, the better the reviews you receive.

Most successful Airbnbers offer their guest more than what is expected to boost their review. A bowl of fruit, chocolates, or small wine bottle might be very appreciated.

Finally, have a guestbook, where guests can leave their comments for you before they leave.

RVShare [39]

If you own an RV that sits in your driveway more than you use it, you might want to check out RV Share [40] which is a site which helps you rent out your RV to others. You can earn passive income by renting it out.

Acorns [41]

Whether you want to get into a "small-change" investment plan is up to you. It only takes a few minutes to join the popular Acorns site. You set up an account and Acorns uses the funds in your account to invest in various investments.

The Acorns app automatically rounds up the purchases you make on linked credit or debit card. For example, say you buy a cup of coffee for $2.75 - Acorns automatically sweeps or takes the change - 25 cents - into a computer-managed investment portfolio. Read the Acorns site [42] for more details.

Acorns charges fees on your account depending on the balance.

Your funds are not insured by the FDIC, but Acorns reports it has Securities Investor Protection Corporation (SIPC) ensuring accounts up to $500,000 which meaning that if Acorns were to become defunct and uncollectible, you would be covered for a maximum of $500,000 (unless SIPC is defunct). Make sure you read all information and reviews before getting into any investment plan.

There are other small investment sites besides Acorns like Betterment [43], and others.

Your earnings should be treated as passive income but be sure to check with a tax advisor on earnings (and tax treatment of losses too) to be sure.

Flippa [44]

Flippa is a site which lists websites for sale. Flippa displays websites for sale showing general monthly income and average visitors/users per month.

Good income producing websites are expensive and if you have the funds, you may want to buy a passive income producing website and later sell it. This may take some expertise so check with your professional advisors (accountants, lawyers, etc.) so you are fully informed before you make any purchase. See the Flippa [45] site for more info and be cautious before buying anything.

*

☺ There are some jokes so dumb they are funny:

Joe walks into a bar and notices there's a basket of peanuts in the shell in front of him. He reaches for one, then hears a voice, "You are an amazing man, Joe. Joe, many people in this community admire you. You are a notable example for everyone in this community. You're good looking too, Joe!"

Joe pulls his hand back and takes a sip of beer wondering about what just happened. He tries to get another peanut and hears, "You are a smart man and a clever man! Hey Joe! Looks like you've been working out too?"

Joe stares incredulously at the basket, then hears several voices,

"Joe, you look so handsome" …. "Whatever you put in your mind to do, you seem to achieve it" …. "Joe, you look very manly today…."

Joe looks over at the bartender and says, "What the hell? There are voices coming out of the peanut basket?"

Bartender says, "Don't worry about it, Joe. The peanuts are complimentary."

SECTION TWO – MANY WAYS TO INCREASE TRAFFIC

Section One of this book discussed ways to create passive online income when you don't have much traffic. This Section discusses ways to increase traffic.

In Section Three, the next section in this book, we give you more ways of earning passive income when you have established extremely good traffic. In Section Four, we give you many and remarkably interesting Active Online Income methods.

We all know you could have the best product, website, or blog on earth, but if people don't know about it you won't have any traffic to your site.

Having traffic enhances passive online income. For example, heavy traffic is necessary to generate online income from sources like AdSense, [46] or YouTube. [47] Passive income commissions from affiliate marketing (i.e. earning commissions on sales you refer your visitors to) increase with the more traffic you have.

Extremely good traffic does not mean tens of thousands of visitors per month, as a large part of those may not be engaging with you. Extremely good traffic means a substantial number of users/visitors (say 5,000 and up per month, for example) if those users/visitors are active and love your site or blog. When you are getting people to post comments on your site, join your mailing list, contact you with questions, etc. means you are getting active and interested visitors.

If you want to have more people learn about you, there are many ways to increase your traffic to your site, blog, articles, etc. Let's begin with discussing ways to generate traffic which will overall help you earn both Passive and Active Online Income.

SEO

Search Engine Optimization or "SEO" means techniques to make your website have a high rank in the search engine pages of Google, Bing, Yahoo and more search engines." [48] This increases the number of visitors to your website. Being able to be found on the first few pages of these search engines will greatly increase your traffic.

If you aren't familiar with SEO techniques (which change from time to time), you can hire private SEO firms to do SEO work on your site for you. There are many private SEO firms that do excellent work, but they are expensive. If hiring a private firm is outside of your budget, you could see what is offered by low-cost SEO contractors on Fiverr [49] or Konker, [50] but you have to be careful in selecting who will do the work for you. If you pick the wrong contractor, it may even backfire on you. It's best to only hire a service which as at least *hundreds* of current favorable reviews and someone who is familiar with current search engine techniques.

Read the reviews and before you order, send a message to the service telling them what you would like them to do, what amount your budget will allow you for this, and any other questions you might have before ordering the SEO service. If they don't deliver, you can request a refund and/or give them a negative review.

Most of the low budget SEO firms will have a description of the services they will do for your site. If you do not understand what they plan to do ask them to explain it to you in simple terms.

For example, "Ozzieuk" is a well-known SEO service who has hundreds of favorable reviews as of the time we are writing this book. We are not endorsing his service in any way, but he does have excellent reviews and serves as an example of a low-cost SEO service with hundreds of favorable reviews. If you are a member of Fiverr, see how Ozzie offers his services as an example only: OzzieUK. [51]

Give the SEO service the keywords you want to rank for and the web page you want to get ranked as one of the top ten sites on Google for those keywords and the geographical area you want to cover.

You can find new keywords if you search your own keywords on Google. For example, say you search "tennis" on Google. You will get a search results page and at the bottom of the page you will see: "Searches related to tennis." Google then shows you eight similar keywords and suggests you may want to search those eight keywords. Use those keywords yourself.

Those keywords are what people type in when they search tennis-related subjects. See if any of the suggested keywords suit you or your product better for SEO purposes.

Also, use the Google AdWords keyword tool or Google keyword planner if you have a Google AdWords account.

Or, you can use other Keyword tools like Keyword Tool [52], or WordStream Free Keyword Tool [53]. There are other keyword tools you can check out by Googling "Free Keyword Tools".

If you pay for SEO, it will take several months to get your site ranked well for highly competitive keywords and less time for long tail keywords. For example, say you have a pizza parlor in Rochester, NY. A highly competitive keyword would be "Pizza Parlor" and a long tail keyword (with less competition) would be "Pizza Parlor in Rochester, NY."

An amazingly simple SEO tactic is to make sure the meta description (the description which appears below the URL in search results) is concise for each of your web pages and has your keywords in it. It will increase each page's rank in search engines and increase your visitors. Consider using "Pizza Parlor in Rochester" in your page meta description. Be accurate on what your page is about as search engines look for keywords not only in the title but in the text as well. So, you would want text on the webpage to again say "Pizza Parlor in Rochester."

Traffic to your site may be increased if you can build up backlinks gradually to your site. Backlinks are links on other sites to your site. Too many backlinks too fast is a negative and may lessen traffic as Google views a quick buildup of backlinks as artificial.

In Google's eyes, the more backlinks a site has to it the more reputable it is, especially if the backlinks come from quality well-known sites. Some SEO experts say a nice long-term goal is to gradually build up (e.g. say 4-5 per week) quality backlinks from reputable sites, but these things change from time to time and it's best to consult with a competent SEO expert.

Anchor text is important in your content. You can use anchor text which will catch the attention of search engines. For example, instead of writing "Google," you can substitute the words, "the number one search engine" on the web which is an example of anchor text.

There is much more to read and learn about SEO and it may be more efficient for you to pay for SEO to help you get more traffic to your site rather than learn more about it yourself as it is time-consuming.

If you want to know where your traffic is coming from, Google Analytics [54] has a support center to help you analyze where your traffic is coming from.

Having proper keywords will increase traffic and the right keywords in the theme of your site will make it easier to find your site. You need have keywords people use to search for your niche. Google's AdWords Keyword tool is one of the most used tools to find the right keywords since it shows what keywords are mostly used by people searching for items in your niche, as well as the "Searches related to…" at the bottom of Google search pages.

To access the AdWords Keyword tool, you may need to set up a Google AdWords account which is free to set up.

Finally, here is a simple SEO Checklist for you. This is not a complete list of all the things you can do to improve your ranking, but it is a start. If you are unable to do the things in this checklist, ask someone to help you, or consider hiring someone.

- o Check your Google search console [55]

- o Use Bing Webmaster tools [56]

- o Use Google Analytics [57]

- o Use Google Suggest which is at the bottom of the Google search page for long tail keywords – When you do a Google Search, Google suggest words will appear below what you have typed in. Or use this keyword tool [58] which is based on google suggest keywords.

- o Use the Google AdWords for their Keyword Planner [59]

- o Make sure you use keywords in the URL for your pages.

- o Use your keyword in the Title of your page, in the first 100 words or so, and in the headings on your page.

- o Use synonyms instead of repeating the same keyword.

- o Use external links to high-quality sites in your text and use internal links to other pages on your site.

o   Check to make sure your page is mobile friendly and use Google's Mobile Friendly Test. [60]

o   Check for any broken links using the free Dr. Link Check [61] and there are other broken link checkers on the net as well.

o   Consider having Hyper Text Transfer Protocol Secure (HTTPS) which is the secure version of HTTP if you don't have it already.

o   Check to see if your pages load fast with Google Page Speed. [62]

o   Get a high-quality inbound link profile using Moz research tool, open site explorer. [63]

o   Name major influencers in your articles and text and let the influencer know about it.

*

Posting in Blogs, Article Writing, etc.

Increasing traffic to your website, by posting on high traffic blogs, and writing articles is an effective way to increase public awareness of your brand.

Keep in mind, it's not complicated to get more traffic. If people like what you do and like your ideas, work, products, etc. they will spread the word and you will get traffic.

Bill Gates wrote, "Content is King," in his well-known 1996 Essay. [64] Gates explained, "The long-term winners are those who used the internet to deliver quality information and entertainment, just like the broadcasting industry."

To be remarkably successful, your content must give real value to your readers, help them to solve problems, build a better life, provide an entertaining experience, give them a great amount of enjoyment, etc. In general, content should provide people with a "BETUM" experience which is:

Beneficial

Entertaining

Thought provoking

Unique & a

Memorable experience

You could have the best SEO Campaign in the world, but if no one likes what you offer, no one will follow you or spend money to get what you are offering.

You don't have to have a lot of money to generate traffic. There are many no-cost ways discussed in this book to increase traffic which you may haven't tried.

Keep in mind, just posting on social media isn't going to do it. You need to produce the right combination of something useful, novel, entertaining, enjoyable, and/or makes life easier or more fun.

You need to have people discover you amongst the vast amounts of posts on the web, and like your content, share it, and spread the word to others so your content goes viral.

Pictures that have inspiring quotes, amazing photos, funny photos, crazy photos, and tremendously beautiful photos tend to go viral.

A short concise solution to a widespread problem tends to go viral. For example, Science Alert posted in 2016 an engaging picture of brain cells with a quote, "New Alzheimer's Treatment" which went viral.

Another example is a picture going viral started on Pinterest with a simple quote and an engaging picture of a man standing on the edge of a cliff in a storm looking down at waters far below next to a waterfall. The picture had the words superimposed on it: "If you want something you've never had, you have to do something you've never done."

Keep in mind if you gradually increase your traffic by making a meaningful presence online your traffic should grow exponentially over time (and remember that takes time).

We will start with discussing some straightforward ways to build up your traffic like posting comments on high traffic sites.

Posting Comments on High Traffic Articles and Blogs

You may already know of blogs in your niche that have a lot of traffic. If not, search on Google for recent high traffic articles and blogs germane to your niche and post intelligent and helpful BETUM comments to readers.

You can find high traffic articles and blogs by first doing a Google search on a subject in your niche, e.g. "tennis books".

After you enter "tennis books" in the google search bar, you will get the first page results. On the first results page, look right below the search box where you entered, "tennis books", and you will see categories in gray for:

"All - Images - New - Maps.... – <u>Tools</u>" (Tools is usually the last one on this line right below the search bar)."

Click on "Tools" and a lower line appears with more categories:

"Any - Country - Any Time - All Results"

Click on the down arrow for "Any Time" and select the "Past Week" or "Past Month". If you are looking for a popular searched subject (such as tennis books), choose "Past Week," and if you are looking for less popular searched items (such as "Tennis books on doing a successful second serve") choose "Past Month".

For tennis books, you then will see a new list of sites visited most by people doing Google searches in the past week on tennis books, or the past month - depending on what "Any Time" choice you just made.

Go through the results and select a few blogs and find articles which allow you to post comments and enter your comments giving attention to who you are.

Don't start trying to sell something in your post. Show your intelligence and consideration for others, and make interesting helpful comments so people get familiar with seeing your posts. Then sporadically, say once every five posts or more, make a reference to your website, product or whatever you feel is proper and not make yourself look spammy. Try extremely hard not to look like your selling your own product and blowing your own horn.

For example, when you want to post a comment calling attention to your Tennis eBook in an Article titled "How to Hit an Awesome Second Tennis Serve," you might comment something like:

"I liked this tennis article very much. I wish I had read it sooner. I struggled for years trying to build a better second serve and had trouble with my toss. I wasn't tossing the ball properly on the second serve, and after I read this article, I learned the correct way to do it. I was so excited after I read it on how easy it was to add speed to my second serve, I looked further and did more research, talked with many tennis teaching pros and I even wrote a book about it (put in the title of your eBook)."

To post comments on high traffic blogs, you usually must become a member. Be sure to read the rules first on the large blogs since most of the exceptionally large blogs don't allow self-serving posts or links to your product, and you will be banned for spamming.

Keep a list of blogs you post comments on and make a schedule for yourself to post weekly (or more often) on the blogs.

BuzzBundle [65]

The BuzzBundle program isn't free. [66] The BuzzBundle software gathers current social media happenings on the keywords you search on the BuzzBundle program. This program makes it extremely easy for you to find, interact and write comments on current social media happenings which are using the keywords you searched for. The program lists those on point happenings, so you can post, interact with other members, and drive traffic to your site.

In other words, the Buzzbundle software directs you to blogs, articles, etc. matching the keywords you give it, and shows you a display of the Articles the program produces. Simply click on the Article and post your comment right into the heart of the discussion. It saves a lot of searching time.

When you become a member of a blog, you need to join with a unique name unlike any others – which helps you stand out. Wiki-how has a 10-step straightforward way to choose a unique name.[67]

*

Joe staggered in the door late in the evening after an afternoon round of golf with several beers, then had a big dinner at a Mexican Restaurant, with 7 more beers and 5 Tequilas to wash it all down.

"I'm bushed honey, I'm going to bed early," Joe said to his wife. He went to sleep but woke up and saw a white-haired man in white flowing robes standing at the end of his bed.

"What the hell? Who are you in my bedroom?" Joe said.

"This isn't your bedroom, Joe. Yes, you guessed it, I'm St. Peter and these are the Pearly Gates."

"What! I can't be dead? Send me back right now!"

"Sorry Joe, it's not that easy. We don't usually send them back, but I can send you back as a cat or a hen. It's your choice," St. Peter said.

Joe thought about it. He didn't like cats, and being a hen didn't seem that great either, but it was his only other choice.

"I want to go back as a hen," said Joe.

Instantly, Joe is on a farm walking around with other hens on a bright sunny day. He likes the sunshine and nice weather and is enjoying himself.

Another hen walks up to him and says, "You must be the new hen St. Peter told us about. How's it going?"

"Well it's okay, but I feel like my ass is about to explode."

"Oh, that's just the ovulation going on, you've got to lay an egg," says the hen.

"Okay," says Joe, "How do I lay an egg?"

"Well, when you feel it coming on, let out a cluck and push."

Joe clucks and pushes. An amazing egg comes out!

"Hey that felt really great," Joe says to the other hen.

Joe feels the urge again, pushes, and another egg pops out!

He does it again, and then hears his wife shouting:

"Joe! Wake up! You're sh#tting all over the bed!

Facebook [68]

You can increase traffic to your site if you share your articles and comments on your Facebook site as well as your other social media. If you belong to Facebook Groups, post your niche articles in the proper niche groups you belong to for added exposure and traffic.

You will be building your audience by sharing your posts with your friends and groups as well.

If you post something about an Influencer (i.e. a major person who writes a lot of tennis books or articles) let the influencer know you like what the

Influencer is doing, and you've written about it. If you send the Influencer a high-quality BETUM article, ask him to share it. Even though people are reluctant to ask others to share since you don't want to inconvenience them, Influencers like to be mentioned – especially in a high-quality post, comment, or article.

If the Influencer shares what you posted, that should magnify the number of shares and give you more traffic.

If you are doing Affiliate Marketing and earning commissions on products of others, share an honest review (a BETUM review) with your Facebook friends of the product and show you are receiving a commission since it's best to be transparent so people will not lose respect for you.

Point out ways the product would be helpful to solve problems or give entertainment and enjoyment. Do posts only about one product at a time to avoid a boring showcasing of many products. Discuss other related products to the one you are reviewing for comparison purposes. Use your affiliate links for the other products as well.

If your friends on Facebook enjoy your niche and you build up a large interest in your FB site, let the manufacturer(s) of the product(s) in your niche know about your FB site and they may decide to pay you a small amount to post more ads or info about their product. It all depends on how much your Facebook site influences others and the quality of your friends.

Start your own Facebook Group to increase public awareness of your brand. The more interesting and entertaining the group is, the more followers you will attract.

Use Your Email Auto Responder Page

Most of us don't normally respond to an email the instant it's received. You can generate more traffic to your site and product(s) by setting up an automatic response to all emails.

To set up an auto response, go to the auto response section of your email and fill in your custom message in the automatic response form.

In your custom message, add something about yourself. For example, your auto response could read, "I will get back to you within 24 hours" (or whatever you decide) and close the message with a short blurb at the end telling them something new in your niche which will benefit them and end your message to them with "Have you read my blog on the brand new easy way to get your first serve in more?"

Change the auto response from time to time to keep it fresh and entertaining. For example, if your niche is magic tricks, you might want to set up an automatic response message that will say:

"Thank you for your interest. Sorry, I'm out briefly now and I should get back to you _____ (e.g., within 24 hours, or however long you want). In the meantime, you ought to see this article on some amazing new magic tricks you can do at parties for lots of laughs > (insert a link to the article or website page you want to share)." Note: If you are doing affiliate marketing – which we discuss later in this book - use your affiliate marketing link whenever you lead someone to a page where they may buy the product. See the FTC FAQs [69] on Affiliate Marketing disclosure. The FTC believes disclosure of a commission affects the weight the reader gives to your review. Seek legal advice on disclosure issues if you have questions.

Then change the response occasionally to read:

"...In the meantime, have you seen our amazing new magic tricks? _____ " < Insert a link to your own magic product or book, i.e., whatever you think will draw attention to your own product and help your sales as well as increase traffic to your site.

Finally, remember to show your website link in your email signature page so everyone you email or respond to, has a link to your site which will increase your traffic.

Share your Facebook Posts in Facebook Groups in Your Niche

Keep in mind, sharing your posts, pictures, videos with FB Groups interested in your niche will increase traffic to your site and your page likes. It's best to only share exciting posts or "BETUM" posts to avoid appearing ordinary or boring.

If enough people in the group share your amazing content, or photos or videos, you will increase your traffic. Amazing posts may go viral as well.

Remember to be link free when you first join and post on a FB group, and don't try to sell anyone anything and abide by the rules. Others in the FB group may report you seeking your removal from the group if you continuously try to sell, sell, sell. This is especially true if you try to sell the group something right away without first taking the time to communicate and get to know other members of the group.

If you see a post from another person in the group that has a need for your services or product, suggest your product in the most interesting way you can without trying to sell it. Something like:

"Yes, I know what you mean (then explain your own experience sincerely and honestly). Then continue with, "This is what helped me (then give them honest information on what you are directing them to view)."

If you begin to stand out in the FB group(s) you joined (you will know if you stand out if other members share and like your posts), consider forming your own group which will again, add more traffic to your website.

You can, of course, pay to boost your post so more people will see your post, but that, of course, costs money.

Another way to spread the word about what you post is to use a Facebook bot to answer messages and do many other things automatically for you. There are many companies like Chatfuel [70] or Botkit, [71] for example, that will help you with a bot. Research these thoroughly before deciding to use these bots. These sites may help you better spread your message.

Cross Promotion of Facebook Groups

If you start your own Facebook Group and gain followers, search Facebook for similar groups in your niche and join them. See if they wish to cross-promote your group with their group, i.e. you promote their group and they promote your new group which will increase your members and traffic as well as their own members and traffic.

Before you suggest a cross-promotion, it's best to offer/share something of value to the members of the other group which they extremely like. For example, run a free or discount promotion for your eBook, or offer your product free or at a discount for one or two days and let only your group and the other group know about it. You can also offer it to the other groups like yours that you would like to eventually do a cross promotion with but let everyone know what you decide to do.

There are many free Kindle Promotion sites, and the well-known book promotion sites usually charge fees. We don't know what your results will be if you try any of these sites, but some book promotion sites have large mailing lists and high page ranks. BookBub is the most well-known and effective if you can get them to promote your book. Here are a few book promotion sites you might want to

73

research. Remember, if you are selling your book on Amazon, follow <u>Amazon Central suggestions for promoting your book.</u> [72]

- o <u>Book Bub</u> [73]

- o <u>Many Books</u> [74]

- o <u>Get Free eBooks</u> [75]

- o <u>eReader News Today</u> [76]

- o <u>Read Cheaply</u> [77]

Try to contact these sites first and discuss your book and genre and see if they can honestly tell you if a promotion of your book will be worthwhile for you. Amazon generally recommends staying within the Amazon recommendations in the Amazon site on selling and marketing your books.

<u>LinkedIn Groups</u> [78]

Consider offering suggestions or links to your LinkedIn connections of new things that would make their lives easier and more enjoyable, and interesting. Intelligent suggestions will also get more people interested in you.

You should also have your LinkedIn profile show how you help other members of LinkedIn. LinkedIn connections are interested in what you offer that will help them at no cost. Review and edit your profile if you have already set one up to show how you help people in your niche.

Your profile is important especially when you request to join a LinkedIn Group. The group may simply base their decision on your profile to see if you would fit well with the group.

For example, you might put a small blurb in your profile that you are passionate about your niche, you continually share news, etc. Show what you reported in the past on the latest tennis equipment, etc. or whatever is popular in your niche.

Going back to LinkedIn Groups, you can easily find groups in your niche on LinkedIn by searching for your niche in the LinkedIn search box in the upper left-hand corner of your homepage. For example, type in and enter the word, "tennis" in the search box and enter and a results page appears. On the results page, you will see several categories appear below the search box:

"All - People – Jobs – Content - … - *Groups*…."

Or, sometimes you will see only a few words appear and the word, "More." If you click on "More" you will get a drop-down menu which has "Groups".

Click on "Groups" and you will get results for all the groups in that niche. Join the groups related to your niche and become a contributing member of the group. Now and then let them know about your website and products how it will help them. Or, like other posts and share other posts and post a comment on helping solve a specific problem someone in the group may be having. Again, it's best not to sell right away.

Think about what would attract the top people in your niche and post that in your profile. For example, you might want to connect with the editor of a large magazine or blog and suggest innovative approaches to increase readership. Most people enjoy a laugh and add clever humor to your request to connect – which might make the editor or his staff curious to investigate it further.

As an example of the use of humor, here is a post we did on Quora. [79]

Or, post articles on your research on common problems editors have and propose solutions. Connect with them as best you can and message them only when you have a BETUM message.

For example, if you want to attract the attention of a tennis magazine editor, look at Tweets and FB posts of various tennis standouts, their coaches, family, etc. and write about them and share them with editors. Editors usually are on the lookout for interesting content.

Also, you can see up to 5 people who have viewed your LinkedIn profile. Viewers of your profile are future potential connections. It doesn't take exceptionally long to see who viewed your profile even if you have a basic free LinkedIn Account – check LinkedIn Help [80] to show you the current way to see who has viewed you. Get in the habit of sending a friendly message to anyone who has viewed you.

LinkedIn Help says you can add up to three websites in your profile. [81] Adding your website to your profile information will increase your traffic.

*

Joe walked into a barber shop and asked for a shave and a shoe shine.

The barber lathered his face and slowly sharpened his large straight edge razor on a leather strap, while a beautiful young woman wearing a very low-cut top knelt down in front of Joe and began to shine Joe's shoes.

Joe's eyes bulged out as he couldn't help himself not staring at her large quivering breasts as she brushed his shoes.

Joe nervously laughed and said to the shoe shine girl, "You and I should get a room."

Completely unfazed, the gorgeous woman said, "My husband wouldn't like that."

Joe said, "C'mon baby, I'll show you a wonderful time!"

Still unfazed, the woman said, "My husband wouldn't like that."

Joe said, "What a waste! Tell your stupid husband you've got to work late, and I'll make it well worth your while."

Unfazed, the beautiful woman continued to brush his shoes, and without looking up said, "You tell him. He's the one shaving you."

Google + Communities

Google Plus Communities [82] are the most used feature on Google+. Communities are groups of members in a niche on Google+. Even though Facebook and others have larger groups, millions are using Google+ communities.

Use the same philosophy as you do with FB groups and LinkedIn groups. Don't sell them right away. Make interesting BETUM comments on the subject matter of the Group and share valuable information with Community Members. Google + allows you to do large posts and add links to all your posts.

Google may put your Google+ posts (especially BETUM posts) to page one of Google search results in your niche as they do this from time to time to attract more people to use Google+.

Instagram[83]

Instagram not only will drive traffic to your site but can be a source of online income to you. If you attract followers with amazing, unique pictures and comments, businesses and other advertisers in your niche may contact you and pay you to advertise their product to your followers.

You don't have to have millions of followers as business marketing departments are more interested in the quality of your followers. 5,000 followers specifically keen on having big tennis serves may be more attractive to advertisers than Instagram accounts with 100,000 followers with varied sports or miscellaneous interests who don't interact.

When you set up an Instagram account, make an attractive profile for yourself. Remember to put a link in your profile to your blog or product since you cannot put links on any of your Instagram images. The link in your profile is the only link allowed on Instagram but will help increase traffic.

You need to describe yourself attractively, interestingly, and briefly, and tell people how following you will help them and give them insight, enjoyment, or entertainment.

You need to create amazing pictures, videos, infographics all conveying your theme to the public to attract followers. Infographics are well-known signs or symbols conveying messages with just an image:

Some examples of what people have done on Instagram are in this Forbes Article on 15 of the top Instagram sites.[84] Some have become very successful.

To attract followers, you should post at least once or twice per day, and at or near the same time(s) each day. You might want to choose 10 am when most people are up and alert, or 5 pm when people are going home, or 7-8 pm when most people are relaxing into the evening.

Every time you add a photo to Instagram you can add text up to 2,000 characters. Write entertaining and engaging text describing the picture or your product or whatever you wish to communicate and attract people with. More people will find your photo based on the amount of text you write.

<u>Instagram has rules on hashtags</u> [85] which change from time to time. Under a recent change, users have the choice now to select, "Don't Show for This Hashtag."

Use around six to nine relevant hashtags or you will appear to be a spammer. Also, if you use too many hashtags, you will look desperate for followers and Instagram frowns on that. Look at other successful Instagrammers in your niche and see what hashtags they use.

If you want to share with other Instagrammers use an @ symbol, followed by their Instagram name. Instagram will notify that Instagrammer of your post and hopefully your post will be shared on and on.

Following people who are interested in your niche or following people who you simply like on Instagram usually leads to you being followed back.

Be aware that Instagram regulates how many people you can follow per day but doesn't publish the exact number. If you go outside their rules, you may be penalized or banned depending on Instagram current rules on their website.

Instagram is social and it's important to respond to as many comments as you can in a friendly and polite manner to people who take the time out to write a comment to your posts. If you converse with people who comment, they may want to share your photos with others, which leads to increased traffic to your site.

The more people comment about your photos shows you are creating something popular which people are interested in; and that you've presented it in a unique way - which will get more traffic to your site.

You should focus on your content more than focusing on getting many followers. Ideally, you want to build a quality list of real followers. So, concentrate on being as creative, unique, and as entertaining as you can. Having a smaller number of engaging followers is much better than a large amount of non-engaging followers.

Don't keep posting requests to people to buy your product as it's better to offer entertainment. Then only bring your product to their attention 10-15% of the time or once every ten days, or so, if you post daily.

You can post up to 60 seconds of video as well. Videos of subjects in your niche will get more comments than a photo, but then again, it's the uniqueness and quality (a BETUM post or video) that decides a successful post.

You can also do an S4S (which means Shout for Shout). A shoutout is a picture of another Instagrammer's profile page shown on your Instagram account. This shows your followers that you support that user and are giving that user added exposure.

Shoutouts usually increase a user's followers. This helps advertisers notice you and perhaps contact you to promote their product or webpage.

Search for Instagramers in your niche with about as many followers as you have, and then contact them to get to know them and vice versa. Everyone is different, but in general, it's best not to request a S4S right away. After commenting back and forth several times, request a S4S if you think it will work.

If you are having trouble with photography, you can easily become a more accomplished photographer and attract more followers (and a resulting increase in your own traffic to your website) by doing some simple adjustments to your photo techniques.

There is a short new excellent book just out by Peter Haraway, "The Absolute Beginner's Guide to

Taking Great Photographs: Quickly and Easily Learn Essential Photography Skills ".[86] This book covers phone cameras as well. We happened to review this book and found it straightforward, useful and practical. There are also many other good books about photography, digital photography, phone cameras, etc.

Pinterest [87]

If you post regularly on Pinterest and get your images out to people and post amazing pictures, you will drive traffic to your site.

You can find trending content by clicking on the hamburger button in the top right-hand corner of the homepage. When you click on the hamburger, you can see what is trending in the "Popular" category. You can also click on other areas such as Health and Fitness, or other subjects to see exactly what is popular in the area you select.

Find an area close to your theme and click on it and you'll find what's most popular and what's generating the most interest and comments. After you look at what is popular on Pinterest, incorporate what's popular in your posts and you will drive traffic to your site or blog.

Haro (Help a Reporter Out) [88]

The HARO homepage describes their well-known site as providing journalists with many sources who can provide the information the journalists need for upcoming stories. And it gives sources opportunities for media exposure.

Through this site, reporters, journalists, and well-known writers from large media companies with a large following request information from people who have inside knowledge on the subject they are writing about.

Join HARO and help a reporter out by showing the reporter how your product/website can exactly enhance and help their story. If the reporter likes your "Pitch", the reporter will use your information and spread the word about your product/website to thousands of readers or more at no cost to you.

For example, say a writer for a popular woman's magazine is looking for new kitchen products, and you've just written a book about new kitchen products, or say you manufacture a new kitchen utensil. HARO allows you to directly message the writer with news about your book/utensil and the writer may decide to use the information you sent.

This, of course, will spread the word about you. That is, if you've helped the writer with quality information _directly related_ to the reporter's request for information, the reporter may mention you in the article which will help you get more traffic all for no cost.

It's free to register on HARO and become a source of content reporters use in their articles. You will receive 3 daily emails from top journalists from media like Reuters, Chicago Tribune, New York Times, ABC News, Time, Wall Street Journal, etc. If the reporter can use your submission, you may get a blurb about your content and website. increase.

HARO maintains the quality of journalists by allowing only journalists from well-known media, or sites with an Alexa site rank of 1,000,000 or less.

HARO has over 35,000 journalists registered with it and over 100,000 sources who receive the daily emails from HARO's journalists requesting information on whatever they are writing about.

The most important thing for you as a source is to become familiar with the rules on HARO before responding to a query from a journalist. The most important rule to follow is to make sure you are directly responding to the journalist's request. For example, if a journalist is requesting suggestions for Valentine Day gifts, you must specifically respond to that and not try to promote your own unrelated product(s) which might not be suitable for Valentine's day (even though your product is new, exciting, and unique). HARO may suspend you if someone reports you as a source who repeatedly doesn't stay within the subject of the request.

Quora [89]

Quora [90] is a well-known and extremely popular site with a remarkably high Alexa rank where anybody can ask questions about anything, and any person who has knowledge of the subject answers the questions. People answering questions can insert engaging diagrams or amazing pictures in their answer as well. Google usually lists Quora Answers on page one of searches relating to the question.

Quora will help you build traffic and give you an opportunity to earn passive online income. If you're an experienced tennis player, for example, you could choose to search out tennis-related questions on Quora and answer the questions.

If you come across an interesting question in your niche on Quora and give a comprehensive (i.e., BETUM) answer adding engaging pictures, thousands may view your answer and increase traffic to your site.

Your answer may be upvoted by readers giving you added exposure and more traffic.

Thousands of people follow certain remarkably interesting questions on Quora and those persons may request notification of any new answers. If you answer much-followed questions in an exciting and intelligent way, your answer may be shown to thousands of the followers.

For example, you can search Quora for "What is the most viewed question in (put in a year)" you will see questions and answers viewed over 1,000,000 times.

And, your answer can continue to attract people to your site for some time if people like your answer and upvote your answer (the top upvoted answers are shown first under the question).

Quora will keep statistics for you on how many people viewed your answer, and Quora may feature your answer in their "Quora Daily Digest" which goes out to over a million people.

Quora's Publishing Team decides on what answers to publish further in their Digest. You can find people on Quora's Publishing Team by looking at the people who answer questions on Quora Publishing. If they are a member of the Quora Publishing Team, it will show they are a member on their profile. See what their areas of interest are and if they are related to your niche you should follow them.

Before answering a question on Quora, review the answers already posted for that question. Most all the top upvoted answers are lengthy and very thorough so make sure you can do likewise before answering. You want to post quality answers to give yourself the best look so that people will want to find out more about you which results in more followers for you and traffic to your site.

Follow people who upvote your answers too and they will usually follow you back which will increase your followers interested in your niche.

Also, if your niche is tennis, view the people who answered tennis questions and follow them, and they may follow you back.

To gain followers:

- o Stick with questions related to your niche.

- o Have a picture of yourself in your profile.

- o Be yourself.

- o Follow anyone who asks you questions.

- o To get noticed more, write answers in a controversial way but make sure you can logically back up your answer with proven facts and reference the proven facts in your answer.

- o Include and link your other social media in your Quora profile.

- o Research other members of Quora in your niche and notice the topics they follow and consider following those topics.

- o Answer high-quality questions.

- o If you don't have time to answer a high-quality question, click on the (…) and you will see an option to answer it later when you have more time.

o Make pictures as interesting as possible and helpful to gain followers. If the images relate to you, explain your personal experience along with your emotions.

o Use your keywords in your answer for Google's search engines.

Other similar Question and Answer sites which generate traffic are StackExchange,[91] Reddit,[92] and others, but Quora is right now the leader in these types of sites.

You don't earn any income by answering questions. Your goal is to become popular in answering questions in your niche. Companies promoting their products will pay you to advertise if you have a large specific following. You will get more traffic as well.

For example, having a good quantity of followers interested in reading your answers to questions relating to tennis could result in your being contacted by tennis equipment manufacturers to advertise their products.

You can further this by letting companies know about your profile when you gain popularity.

Answering questions which help others is a wonderful thing to do since occasionally thousands of people view your answers. Once you start to promote one product, others may ask you to advertise their products and so on depending on how popular you become.

Keep in mind, Quora allows you to choose your interests and Quora will send you questions to answer and other readers also will send questions to you steadily.

You can also post links to the answers you post on Quora on your other social media sites to help your exposure and increase your traffic. Be sure to post any of you Quora answers that get a high number of viewers.

The more questions you answer with high-quality answers, the more you will be recognized and trusted as an excellent source which will attract interest and followers and give your site more traffic. And, answer questions regularly 3 to 4 times a week or more to keep your followers informed and interested.

Become familiar with all Quora rules as Quora frowns on posting self-serving material or your own links to your own products. If you do post links to your products, Quora may ban you if Quora or someone else reports you.

People need solutions to their problems when they don't know how to solve them, and Quora has been an excellent way for people to get answers.

Quora can be used to research current trends. Research current questions which people ask. For example, you may see thousands of people wanting to know more about Bitcoins. You may decide to research Bitcoins and write an eBook about Bitcoins if it is in your niche.

Or, if you see a lot of people trying to find answers on keeping fit or losing weight because of a certain issue like lack of time to exercise, eating large portions, etc.), you may decide to write a book on a solution to it such as "Quick High Intensity Interval Training Methods," or an eBook on ways to reduce portions when eating, etc.

If you are an IT expert, or in another related service industry, you might want to share your ability and knowledge on Quora. People will seek you out for your help and expertise with technical matters.

*

When Joe was a young single man, he played golf every Saturday with his usual group. He and every other guy at the club admired an extremely attractive and sexy single woman who usually practiced by herself on the driving range at the same time Joe's group teed off.

Joe lusted for her. Crazily infatuated with this woman, Joe wanted to meet her desperately. He deeply desired to talk to her but he was shy when he saw her. And nervous too. He just couldn't get his courage up to say hello to her.

He looked around the golf club for her every time he was there. He asked about her, but no one knew who she was. Joe spent sleepless nights thinking how he could approach this gorgeous woman.

One-night Joe had a dream. In the dream, he was hitting balls on the practice range but this time he pulled out of his golf bag a magic bright fluorescent

95

orange driver, brighter in color than any driver he'd ever seen. It looked magnificent. In his dream, Joe instantly appeared on the driving range hitting golf balls with the orange driver farther than he'd ever hit golf balls in his life.

While he was hitting huge shots with his magic driver, the beautiful woman approached him.

"Excuse me." She said. "I couldn't help but notice the orange driver you are using. You are hitting it very well!"

"Oh, hello! You are very welcome to try it yourself. Here try it and you'll be amazed by the difference in distance," Joe said. Joe politely handed her the driver and she smiled and tried it. Sure enough, the gorgeous woman hit balls even further than Joe.

After several shots, they began to talk, and Joe politely introduced himself. "My name is Joe. I've seen you here practicing every Saturday and wanted to meet you. But no one here at the club seems to know who you are?"

"Oh, yes. My name is Vanessa." Her sweet sexy voice made Joe yearn with desire. Vanessa continued talking to Joe in his dream, and Joe focused on her beautiful red lips as she mouthed her words to him in a dreamy slow motion.

Vanessa paused hitting more balls and said to Joe, "I'm cursed with being so attractive. Men keep bothering me -- interrupting me. I try to keep to myself, it's better that way. The attention I get is sooo annoying."

"Aaah, you have my sympathy, and I understand exactly how you feel. A true gentleman like myself understands how annoying that can be to a beautiful woman like yourself. You certainly are a great golfer and incredibly attractive. My sister has the same problem – fighting away men all the time. Here, why don't you practice with this driver more and I'll hit over there. If you want to borrow it for a week or more, that would be fine with me. Just give it back to me when you're finished. For now, I'll stand here so no one will bother you."

"Why thank you! You are a gentleman and a genuinely nice person."

Joe smiled and after the beautiful woman finished hitting Joe's magic driver they began to talk more, and they got along so well, Joe asked her out for dinner and she happily accepted.

They went to dinner and had a wonderful time getting to know each other. Dreaming Joe was in love.

"Briiinggg!" Joe's alarm went off and he jumped out of bed. Today was Saturday and he didn't waste any time getting his driver and carefully painted the head on his driver a bright fluorescent orange and rushed out with the orange driver early to the range and began to hit balls just as he did in his dream. Then Joe noticed the gorgeous woman was now walking up to hit balls on the range. Just like in his dream, the gorgeous woman noticed the orange driver and went up to talk to Joe.

"Excuse me." She said in a sweet voice. "I couldn't help but notice the orange driver you are using. You are hitting it very well!"

"Yes!" Joe said. Then Joe began with a throaty, nervous laugh, like that sound a dog makes just before it throws up and said, "Do you want to f#ck?"

PPC Ads

You can, of course, pay for advertising which will bring people to your site or to your product page. However, once you stop the ads, your traffic falls off. Ads do work as long as you select the right places to advertise such as Facebook Ads,[93] Twitter Ads,[94] LinkedIn Ads,[95] Google AdWords Express,[96] Bing Ads,[97] and Amazon Ad Campaigns.[98]

You need to study and research where your potential buyers are. For example, if you are selling Amazon products FBA,[99] the best and most obvious place to set up ads is on the Amazon site itself (since that is where millions of Amazon shoppers hang out). You use Amazon Ad Campaigns [100] to attract Amazon shoppers to your FBA products, and any other products such as eBooks, Paperback Books, Apps, Music, Audio Books, etc. which you put up for sale on Amazon.

Invite Market Influencers to Guest Blog

Increase your traffic by inviting Influencers and other experts in your niche to guest blog on your site. They may reciprocate and share your site on their blog which will bring more traffic to your site. Or, you can ask them to answer interview questions and then post the interview on your site with a link back to them.

Most experts want to spread the word about themselves, so it doesn't hurt to email them and politely ask them if they would answer a few interview questions for a featured interview on your site. Explain to them how it would be helpful to them. Influencers usually have highly specialized niches and they don't like to hear about anything that is not related to their specific niche.

Influencers are busy and want relevance, value, appreciation, personality, and relationships which are mutually beneficial. Think about what you can offer them that is related to their specific niche.

Follow up later with more specific information and ask if they would be interested in posting a blurb about you and your site.

Link Your eBook to Your Site and Use Kindle Select [101]

Put a link to your site in your eBook and put your book on the Kindle Select eBook Enrollment for 90 days which allows your book to be loaned free for 14 days to thousands of readers. [102]

As a further promotion, you can offer your book for free during the 90-day Kindle Select period furthering the spread of your website.

Build Your Email List

An excellent way to get more traffic is to build up an email list and send a Newsletter to them.

There are many email services like MailChimp [103] which has been in business since 2001 and they make it easy for a beginner to build an email list and send out regular newsletters. If you use MailChimp read about email list regulations as you don't want to be a spammer.

Also, Mail Chimp has an Article about the new General Data Protection Regulation effective May 25, 2018. [104]

There are many things you can do to have people join your email list.

You can do a giveaway of your product in exchange for people subscribing to your email list.

You can create an engaging and interesting Quiz and award a prize using Qzzr.com. [105] Having people take an engaging quiz and awarding a free copy of an eBook or informational pdf to those in your niche who correctly do the quiz is a great way to get traffic to your product and sign up for your Newsletter.

The Qzzr.com site does cost money, but it will help you create engaging quizzes. Qzzr offers a free trial so you can see if it will be useful for you.

Challenge everyone to share the Quiz to see if they can beat their friends in doing the quiz.

In general, you can offer anything of informational value to people who share an interest in your niche in exchange for their email address.

It's not good to share email lists with someone else's email list in your niche, since you may be violating privacy laws. Check with your legal advisor to get current information on sharing private email addresses.

To promote your Newsletter, post, and comment on high traffic blogs on something of great interest to everyone in your niche. Tell them there is more information available in your newsletters and provide a link or a mention of where they can subscribe to your newsletter.

Use testimonials from others who received help from your newsletter and post a convenient newsletter sign up near the testimonials.

On your email registration form, just ask for an email address or their first name since people protect their information and want privacy.

If you belong to local groups related to your niche, exchange business cards to learn their email address and ask them if it would be all right for you to email the information. Give them your card first before asking. Have your business card contain information on how they can get something free from you related to your niche by signing up for your newsletter.

If you are selling products on your site, offer discounts or free information only to subscribers.

SECTION THREE – CREATING PASSIVE ONLINE INCOME WHEN YOU *DO* HAVE TRAFFIC

YouTube [106]

You need a large following or people familiar with what you do on the web to get a good start on building a YouTube Channel for your services and/or products. So, notify everyone on your email lists, your contacts on your email accounts, Facebook friends, LinkedIn Connections, Instagram Followers and all your social media groups you've created a YouTube Channel and tell them what it is about and give them the link to it.

Send them a teaser video for your channel or something of value common to your niche if they subscribe to your channel. For example, make one of your eBooks free for three days and tell them to download it as a goodwill gesture and for taking the time to read about your new YouTube Channel.

YouTube has over a billion active users. A simple example of an extremely popular YouTube Channel is PewDiePie, a young Swedish man, whose real name is Felix Kjellberg, who has over 50 million subscribers.

He's in his late twenties now and has a net worth estimated at 90 million dollars, all earned primarily through YouTube. He is a comedian and makes people laugh from his energetic, silly, profane but genuine and realistic content.

You can create a YouTube account and channel for free. When you create your account, put in keywords describing the theme of your channel to help people find you. See the SEO pages in Section Two of this book for finding and using the right keywords.

Keep your channel name simple and catchy so people will remember you if they like your channel.

Then create your videos and put them on your channel. Your videos must be your own work and you can't use any copyrighted material.

There is a lot of competition, so you want to do high-quality videos with what you have available, and again, "Content is King." The better your content, the more success you will have. Stay within your theme so the people who subscribe to your channel will stay with you. Be imaginative and consistent to your niche.

Another example of a successful YouTube Channel is, "<u>Fitness Blender</u>" [107] created by a husband and wife, Daniel and Kelli. Both are exercise gurus and they offer over 500 free exercise videos of high quality, including training programs. They have videos on cardio, core, strength, balance, and general fitness which are effective and produce visible results and have millions of subscribers.

They offer free fitness advice during the videos as well. People found they got results from doing the videos and word spread. Their channel is an excellent example of how an average couple with a high interest in fitness can be successful on YouTube with excellent content.

They regularly update with new videos to keep their followers interested. Their exercise videos appeal to a wide range of people from early age to seniors and range from simple low-impact exercises to insane, brutal, gut-busting one hour 1000 Calorie burn workouts.

We noticed there are many other YouTube Channels with extreme workouts, and the popularity of Fitness Blender seems to come from the wide range of exercise workouts they offer for all ages with free physical training advice.

Daniel and Kelli also interact with their followers by asking them for input and create new videos accordingly.

They reply to their comments, emails, and create videos thanking them or responding to their frequently asked questions.

Another example of a successful YouTube Channel is a very well-known Channel known as Dc Toy Collector which made $4 million dollars in one year simply showing a pair of women's hands opening boxes of toys. This channel effectively entertained babies and toddlers quieting them down giving many mothers a much-needed break when trying to handle all their energy.

Passive income comes from the ads put on your YouTube Channel. Give a lot of thought on what you want your YouTube Channel to give to people.

Research your competition to see what they do and the quality of their videos.

Once you have created your own channel and built up a following, you can monetize your YouTube channel by having advertisements at the beginning of each video and which generate revenue for you each time the ad is viewed.

YouTube makes it easy to monetize your site and you simply click on the "monetize with ads" button when you upload your video which will add advertisements automatically to your video.

If you haven't monetized earlier videos, you can do that by clicking on the $ sign on the side of the video and click on the "monetize with ads" button.

In addition to monetizing your YouTube site, you can set up a Google AdSense[108] account (it's free to set up) which will place ads during your video. Google will pay you through your PayPal account when people click on your ads. If you don't have a large following, it is exceedingly difficult to generate revenue through ads.

Finally, once you have many followers and videos, you might want to join the YouTube Partner Program where you earn money per thousand views of your video rather than the tiny amounts earned from very few clicks.

Affiliate Marketing and YouTube

Affiliate Marketing means you earn money online by promoting the products of another company for a commission on each sale you make. So, in theory, all you must do is collaborate with affiliate programs, get their affiliate links, and start promoting them on your channel.

Affiliate Marketing is alive and well on YouTube where you earn commission from sales of products shown on your YouTube Channel.

The products should relate to your theme, and many people create YouTube "Review" videos giving honest research results and an intelligent analysis of the product with a link to where the viewer can buy the product. People tend to give a helpful review for anything they think will sell. But if your review is not a quality and honest review, people won't read your future reviews of other products.

You should get competent legal advice on disclosing you are receiving a commission on a product review. See these <u>FTC FAQs</u> [109] on disclosure and full disclosure shows your honesty and transparency which will help people respect your opinion.

Affiliate Marketing

Affiliate marketing is passive income generated by earning commissions from referring people to sites where they can buy the product. There are several very large affiliate marketing programs which are free to join such as <u>Clickbank</u>,[110] <u>Amazon Associates</u>,[111] <u>eBay Partner Network</u>,[112] <u>Walmart</u>,[113] <u>AliExpress</u>,[114] <u>ShareaSale</u>,[115] <u>CJ Affiliate</u>,[116] <u>DigiResults</u>,[117] and others.

It's best to stay with well-known quality affiliate sites when you first start out to hopefully avoid problems like affiliate hijacking where you aren't given credit for your referral.

People who have products list their products with these sites and get increased exposure for their product.

Normally if you are passionate about your niche and have products related to your niche, you get a lot of enjoyment from doing what you love to do. If you select a niche which is not as popular (e.g. collecting dead beetles?) as other niches it may be difficult to generate a lot of income in relation to the time you put in.

Remember the three largest and time-tested niches in affiliate marketing products are:

1. Health & Fitness

2. Dating and Relationships

3. Making Money and Business

If you love these areas and work your niche in one or more of these areas, you will reach more people more easily.

Clickbank is explained in more detail in the next sub-section. Clickbank helps you to become a product creator where you advertise your product to thousands of affiliates offering them a high commission if they sell your product. Clickbank features informational products like a new diet or lessons on how to become an expert at something.

It is free to become a Clickbank affiliate member and when Clickbank approves you, Clickbank assigns a code to you, so you will be known as the one who referred the customer and you will earn a commission if they buy it.

If you want to sell your product on Clickbank, there is a cost (an "activation fee" of about $50). The small activation fee seems reasonable since you are putting your product out for thousands of affiliates to sell it for you.

Clickbank is a massive site. Study it well and become very familiar with it before you start to sell on Clickbank. Research what products are selling and what products aren't selling, and why.

Be sure you are referring products of excellent quality. If the product turns out to be inferior quality, it will be a bad reflection on you and people will lose interest in you.

Disclose you are getting a commission for products you refer people to or products you might recommend in an article. See the FTC Endorsement Rules [118] (which promote transparency, and FTC rules change from time to time). Seek professional legal advice if you are in doubt.

If your website is running on WordPress there is a new plugin, Insta Econ Express,[119] which uses

content spinners to automatically build a
WordPress Affiliate Marketing Website very quickly.
You just need to fill in the types of products and the
program will build the site very quickly for you. You
then edit it to your liking. This only works with sites
with WordPress installed.

Clickbank [120]

Clickbank offers thousands of products to affiliate
marketers and you can become one of the
thousands of affiliate marketers on Clickbank
selling Clickbank products. You can also obtain
your own product and sell it through thousands of
other affiliate marketers on Clickbank.

If you are interested in selling Clickbank products,
pick a product relevant to your niche. The average
product costs around $40 and commissions are
high and can range up to 90% but most
commissions are in the range of 50% to 70%.

Use your coded Clickbank link in selling products
on your site, your YouTube Channel, blogs, articles,
and social media.

Clickbank products tend to be informational
products that solve problems. Clickbank shows you

what products are selling, but review as many products as you can. You might come across one little-known product specific to your niche which your followers would love to get. If the word spreads, the product may become popular and it's nice to be on the ground floor.

Review the product first yourself and try to get a "sales copy" of the product and decide whether it is right for you to promote.

If you are writing a review article on the product you wish to sell, keep in mind a series of articles may give you more exposure. Once you've written one review, write another review on the product or divide your review up to two or three pieces and publish a week apart.

If you want to sell your own product on Clickbank, see this Clickbank support page [121] on how to effectively sell your own product by using a Pitch Page and a Thank You Page.

Amazon Associates [122]

Before discussing Amazon Associates [123]in detail, know Amazon has an exceptionally large affiliate program for website owners. Amazon must first approve your website before accepting you as an affiliate to sell Amazon products.

If a visitor to your website clicks on a link to a product on Amazon, you earn a commission on that product. If the visitor decides not to buy it, you still earn a commission on anything else which the shopper puts in their shopping cart since your site originated their visit to the Amazon site.

If a visitor goes through your site to buy an inexpensive product on Amazon but instead puts in his shopping cart a large expensive item like an electronic device on sale, or an Ultra HD Smart TV you earn a commission. *Best websit Wix.WU*

We assume you know about building your own website via WordPress [124] or GoDaddy [125] or other similar sites. If not, visit a website building site and become familiar with creating a website – it is getting easier as time goes on.

Once you have your website up and running and build up traffic to your niche site, you can begin affiliate marketing. One way to build up traffic to a new site is to write a brief quality review on a hot trending niche product and then having a link to your website where people can learn more about the product on your website. You post more information about the product on your site and use your affiliate link supplied by Amazon Associates to the Amazon page of the product. If the potential buyer buys the product, you will get a commission. And, if the buyer buys more products and puts additional products in her shopping cart, these sales will generate a commission for you.

Look for high priced items to review (over $200 that are trending and popular) and look for low-cost trending and popular items to review as well. You will sell a more of the low-priced items than high priced items. Sales of low priced items show your reviews are being read and appreciated. Remember to write quality reviews and make sure you fully research the product and read existing reviews posted on Amazon about the product as well.

To maximize your commission, your goal would be to write interesting and content-rich reviews of high priced trending items and get a volume of sales of low priced items. Try to keep your reviews from 300 words to 500 words – enough content to create interest and not too long to avoid losing a reader.

Post the review on your website and share the article on Social Media Groups and Communities,

Quora, and other methods discussed in the Traffic Section of this book to get traffic.

You should have a call to action at the end of your review such as, "See other reviews on this product" or "Buy Now", etc. and have your Affiliate link to your site where you have additional information or further reviews of the product, and then an Amazon affiliate link on your site leading to the Amazon page of the product on Amazon.

Become familiar with Amazon Associate rules since Amazon doesn't allow their affiliate links sent via email to your email list, but rules change from time to time.

eBay Partner Network [126]

eBay's Affiliate Marketing program is called the "eBay Partner Network." See this eBay video showing how their affiliate marketing program works. [127]

If you already have an eBay account, you just need to add a bit more information to join their program. eBay pays commissions on "Qualifying Transactions" which they define as, "A transaction which occurs when (1) an end user makes a

117

purchase within 24 hours after clicking your link for a "Buy It Now" item, or (2) an end user places a bid on an "Auction" item within 24 hours after clicking your link and wins that auction within 10 days."

You receive a percentage of the revenue eBay earns, and eBay explains there are some items where there is extraordinarily little or no eBay revenue earned like gift cards, items sold by charities, and special promotional deals.

Walmart [128]

Walmart provides banners and text links for affiliates to anything on Walmart.com and gives you access to banners and newsletters for a wide selection of items to post on your site.

You earn commissions on purchases of products originating from your site. Walmart must first approve your site.

AliExpress [129]

The commissions vary on AliExpress and change from time to time and the commissions begin at 5%

and go up from there. It's easy to join and they also provide incentives and tools to help you with marketing.

ShareASale [130]

ShareASale has been in business for 18 years and has mostly small to midsize merchants who sign up with ShareASale for its Affiliate network.

ShareASale allows their affiliates freedom to market their merchant's products and affiliates can use their own website, blogs, social media, PPC campaigns, SEO campaigns, RSS, email, and other methods.

CJ Affiliate [131]

CJ Affiliate has been in business for 20 years and serves "Advertisers" who want to sell their products through CJ (formerly known as "Commission Junction"). "Publishers" is the term used for affiliate marketers that join the CJ network.

CJ operates worldwide and describes their network as, "Working with many Internet Retailer 500 companies - double the amount our competitors have, and our affiliates (CJ calls them "Publishers"), have access to top brands in one account in our network."

DigiResults [132]

DigiResults offers an innovative approach to Affiliate Marketing where DigiResults has Vendors and Affiliates paid at the point of sale through their PayPal accounts. They explain on their website, "Unlike other networks that take weeks or even months to get paid, you start earning, from your very first sale."

As far as refunds go, they allow vendors to set their own refund policies and handle all refunds automatically through their Direct Commission Technology.

If the vendor is offering a 50% commission, the vendor gets paid 50% and the Affiliates get paid 50% all at the point of sale.

Everbuying [133]

Everbuying has been in business since 2006 and is like Aliexpress. Everbuying features Chinese wholesale products. They describe themselves as a leading China wholesale shopping site. They go on to explain they feature electronics and current fashions which are top quality. And they try to provide them at the lowest prices. They want affiliates with high traffic.

*

Joe and his wife, Jane, were celebrating their wedding anniversary at the golf clubhouse dining room.

"Jane, I was wondering if you ever were unfaithful to me over the years," Joe said.

"Oh, Joe, I don't want to talk about…"

"Jane, I really want to know."

"Oh, all right. Three times."

"Three? Okay, when were they," asked Joe?

"Well Joe, remember when we first got married you really needed a loan and no bank would touch you? Well, remember the chief bank loan officer came over to the house with a check for you and had you sign all the loan papers?"

"Oh, Jane, you did that for me? I think even more of you now…but when was the second time?"

"Remember when you had your heart attack and were close to death? No one wanted to do the heart surgery on you. Then the best cardiac surgeon in town suddenly appeared and operated on you?"

"Oh, gosh Jane, I love you very much. You saved me from dying. So, when was the third time?"

"Well, Joe, remember last year when you wanted to be the Golf Club Captain here at this club and you were 27 votes short?"

AdSense [134]

You can earn passive online income from advertisements via Google's AdSense program if you have a lot of traffic.

Google puts advertisements on your site and you earn a small amount when visitors click on the ads. The reason you earn is that Advertisers pay Google if someone clicks on the ad (i.e. PPC) and Google pays you a percentage of what they are paid from the advertiser.

For example, advertisers pay Google say $.50 cents per click. Google pays you 70% or $.35 cents per click.

Advertising income is simple passive income if you are getting high traffic. Google takes care of placing the ads on your website which are related to the theme of what your visitors are interested by your website's theme.

You can choose the places where the ads will appear. You should consider placing the places for ads on your first page above the fold, so they can see the add when someone visits your site.

To get other ideas of where you should place ads on your web pages, research and view your competitors' sites and see where they place their ads. Google Support also makes recommendations on the places for ads on your website. [135]

Media.Net [136]

Media.net is like Google's AdSense program. Media.net runs Yahoo and Bing Ad searches.

Using ad networks like AdSense doesn't prevent you from using other ad networks as well.

You can search the web for potential manufacturers, businesses, associations, and other advertisers who sell products relevant to your niche and you can offer them advertising packages. If you take direct advertising from them, they may want you to give traffic reports which you can get through Google Analytics. [137]

Infolinks [138]

Infolinks will also place ads on your site and at the time of this writing, Infolinks is the third largest ad technology platform.

Hubpages [139]

Join HubPages and earn ad revenue from people clicking on ads on the webpage your article appears on the HubPages site.

The more popular your article, the more you earn. If you don't get people reading your article, you won't earn very much. So, chose to write an original article (a BETUM article) on trending topics to make it easier to get a lot of traffic. HubPages only accepts original articles. It is a large site and here are HubPages FAQs which explain HubPages. [140]

The higher the quality of your article and the closer your article follows HubPages recommendations, the more traffic you will generate for your article.

Once you publish your article on HubPages, don't stop there as it doesn't take long to promote your article on all your social media to get more people to visit your article on HubPages.

InfoBarrel [141]

InfoBarrel is like HubPages and the more popular your articles are, the more you will earn. Last time we checked, InfoBarrel pays through PayPal at a slightly higher percentage than HubPages but review both sites before submitting your article for publication.

Medium Partner Programs [142]

You can also publish an original article on Medium. This is a new site that doesn't pay you based on ad revenue from clicks. You earn based on your reader engagement which is measured by how many "claps" are given to your article.

Remember this site is new and read all the rules before you use this platform for your articles.

*

Joe was hitting golf balls on a range trying to get the attention of Gary Player who was hitting on the other side of the range. Every time Gary Player would hit a ball Joe would hit if further then Joe looked at Gary to see if he was impressed.

Gary would hit a fade then Joe would hit a higher and more perfect fade even further, and so on. This started to annoy Gary, so he waved Joe over to him.

"You hit some impressive shots for a youngster. I was wondering if you've got your tour card yet."

"Well, ah, I could get it any time, I was leading in the last three qualifiers but thought, hey, it's too easy. All that travel? Nope, not for me. Yeah, that's right. I could qualify any time I choose. But, I'm going to have fun before I get into that grind." Joe said.

Player stared at him, and then said, "You know I've designed many golf courses, and I could get you a job at one of the most exclusive courses I've ever designed. They pay around $200k for a new assistant pro. And, the course is owned by a very wealthy old man who is looking for a chauffeur and a bodyguard for his beautiful granddaughter and you'll have to see to all her needs."

"Wow, that sounds great!" Joe said.

"You're young and very tall and I assume you've got a strong sex drive, because from what I hear, and I don't mean to be awkward but, you're going to need it with this job."

"Yeah, yeah, I can do that!" Said Joe, now getting very excited.

"Well you'll have to fly over to South Africa to meet everyone, but the owner will send his jet for you and his granddaughter will come to meet you. She's in her early 20s and she's got one hell of a sex drive. Oh, and you'll have to escort her on all her trips," said Gary.

Joe was wide-eyed, and said, "You bullshittin' me?"

Gary replied, "Yeah, well.... You started it."

SECTION FOUR – EARN ACTIVE ONLINE INCOME

Active online income means you spend your time actively earning money from online sources vs. passive online income methods where your product – like an eBook, for example – earns money itself after you spent time creating it.

You are putting in your time and effort to earn active income using your skills. In other words, active income is income you earn in exchange for your time and service. Examples of active income are wages, salaries, and money you earn from your active participation in earning the money.

There are many online ways to actively earn money instead of getting a job with an established company and going to work every day at the same desk or workplace.

We will first discuss opportunities to earn money using mobile apps which you can easily put on your phone.

Mobile Apps

People earn active income conveniently and quickly by using Mobile Apps. If you are willing to put in your time and effort you may want to try these. For most of these apps, all you need is your phone.

Swagbucks [143]

Swagbucks at the time of this writing has paid over $175 Million to members. [144]

If you sign up for a Swagbucks free account and download the app to your phone, that is all you need to do to earn active income.

You take part in surveys, browse the internet (which may be something you do anyway). Swagbucks is exceedingly popular and easy to use. If you get friends to sign up, you earn bonus points and they will get a $5 reward for joining.

Other income generating survey apps
Crowdology [145] MySurvey [146]

Crowdology is free to join and will pay you a small amount to complete surveys. Some of the surveys are very long and if the survey is a long one, you will get paid more.

MySurvey pays you in rewards and points. The rewards are vouchers you can redeem like Amazon vouchers. The points can be redeemed for cash to your PayPal account.

EasyShift [147]

Businesses sometimes need to get a look into shopping scenes and through EasyShift, businesses pay people to go in and take photos of their displays, etc. They will pay you within 48 hours after you complete your shift.

You can get the EasyShift app here [148]

FlexJobs [149]

If you are looking for a job that will fit around your lifestyle instead of a job which you fit your lifestyle around, check out this app. FlexJobs was created by a woman who wanted a job that would fit around her family life.

The people who use Flex Job can search over 50 categories of jobs for people who want to work at home part time or full time.

FlexJobs report that of these 50 job categories, the following 10 job categories are on the rise: [150]

- o If you like to Edit there are jobs on FlexJobs for Editing, Copywriting and Copy Editors.

- o If you like to write, there are jobs for Technical Writers, Resume Writers, and General Writing.

- o There are Data Entry jobs such as Data Entry Clerk, Quantitative Market research, etc.

- o Advertising jobs.

- o Event Planning jobs are on the rise for Event Coordinator, Event Assistants, Event Planners.

- o If you like Journalism, there are jobs for News Writers, News Editors, and News Producers.

- o It's no surprise Internet & Ecommerce jobs are in demand, such as jobs for Social Media Coordinators, and eCommerce Managers, and Digital Strategists.

- o Account Manager jobs are on the rise and Sales Reps.

- o Of course, Computer & IT jobs are rising such as project managers, systems engineers, and analysts.

- o Accounting and Finance jobs are on the rise as well for Bookkeepers, accountants and accounting clerks.

In general, the people who use FlexJobs want:

- o Career orientated part-time jobs.

- o Freelancers looking for more work, projects, and clients.

o Homemakers who want a flexible job to fit around family life or other projects.

o People who want to supplement their income where they use their skills to the fullest.

o People in rural areas where few jobs are available and who don't want to move.

o Disabled people with physical disabilities.

o Retirees who want extra income.

You must pay to join the site for at least one month at around $15 per month and it's less expensive to join if you choose to join for a longer term.

Before joining, you can view and search the jobs to see exactly what jobs are available, but you must join to apply for any jobs.

Checkpoints [151] "The App That Pays You Back"

You earn through Checkpoints by scanning barcodes, taking quizzes, watching videos, and surfing the web.

You get points and you redeem the points for prizes. Checkpoints has a <u>video</u> [152] which explains their app which makes it easy to understand what you have to do to earn points toward free prizes, etc.

Field Agent App [153]

The Field Agent app enables you to earn money by completing easy jobs like checking stock and store displays. You complete the task at your convenience and you don't have to work a shift like EasyShift and you are not required to be available for the shift at a specific time. Field Agent pays you by PayPal.

Gigwalk [154]

Again, active income comes from putting your time and effort in to earn money. It is actively earning money for your services, wages, a set fee job, etc. Gigwalk is a notable example of earning Active Income. Gigwalk explains their app like this:

- o A Gigwalk client posts work as "Gigs" and these gigs appear as a gig list on a map displayed on your mobile phone or other online devices you may have.

- o You view the map and find Gigs in your area that you can perform well.

- o Pick a gig and apply. There is an "Apply to this Gig" button to click on.

- o A notification is later sent if you've been selected and if so, the details of the job with instructions are sent to you online.

- o You complete the work and tell Gigwalk you've completed it through the Gigwalk app.

- o The client checks your work and approves it and you are paid directly to your PayPal account.

Gigwalkers [155] do jobs like taking pictures of an intersection or roadblock, photographing hours of operation of a business, etc. The types of Gigwalk gigs are endless as anyone or any business needing information can post a gig and set the price for completing the gig.

WorkLLama [156]

After downloading the app, WorkLLama [157] allows you to find and work - any type of work that suits you and your schedule. You can instantly view what is available after you download the app. It is up to you to choose the work, who you chose to work for, where you work, and when you work.

You can search by job type, industry, skills, pay, and when you start. WorkLLama's app is designed to help you find work is suited to you.

TaskRabbit [158]

This app gives you information on jobs in your area relating to moving, making deliveries, repair person jobs, hand-assemble furniture, lamps, bicycles, BBQs, etc.

People who use TaskRabbit seek Taskers to do jobs on a certain day and time when they want the Tasker to show up to do the work.

Anyone who signs up to work as a Tasker must pay a registration fee for a background check and go through an orientation before getting connected to work or jobs in their area.

Once approved, Taskers then use the app to find local work and book tasks with people who want tasks done in the area. After the tasker completes the job, the Tasker sends an invoice for payment.

You set your own rates and you can post your rates for different jobs. Keep in mind there is a lot of competition, and there is a commission to pay to TaskRabbit.

DogVacay [159]

In the past, most people who travel left their dogs in a kennel. Today, people who want an alternative to a kennel use a private person to take care of their dog while they are away.

You can earn money taking care of dogs. If you do it well, there is usually a lot of repeat business. You choose the breed of dogs, age, weight, etc. and set your own rates.

You create a profile for yourself and let people know when you are available to take pets.

There is competition, of course, and a 20% service fee. You set your own rates for overnights, and any other pet services like dog walking, grooming, and whatever you offer in addition to overnight stays.

Mobee [160]

On Mobee you become a secret shopper for well-known stores in your area. After completing a secret shopper mission, you earn points which can be used on a wide choice of gift cards or rewards.

You decide what missions you want to go on and send your review of your experience by answering questions which the business then uses to gain knowledge on their own service and sometimes their competitors' service.

AppTrailers [161]

AppTrailers is a way of earning reward points redeemable for gift cards in Amazon, Starbucks, and others or paid via PayPal. You simply view trailers on new apps and report if you understood it or not. See the site for more details.

*

Joe and Jane got divorced but Joe missed her and bought Jane the high-performance car she always wanted. They were driving to a shopping center on a dark and stormy night and Jane crashed killing them both. They woke up finding themselves in front of the pearly gates of Heaven.

They realized they were dead. They reconciled while waiting for St. Peter to open the gates and still loved each other and wondered whether they could get married in heaven by a Catholic priest. St. Peter walked up and greeted them with his laptop in hand.

"St. Peter," Joe said, "We were wondering if we could get married in heaven?"

St. Peter shook his head, "I don't think we've ever had two people get married in heaven. Wait here, I'll check."

St. Peter went away, and weeks passed. Huge long lines of people waiting to get into heaven started to form. St Peter was nowhere to be found.

Joe and Jane wondered what was going on. They start to have second thoughts about getting married again, thinking they might not get along in the eternity ahead. They could have problems with their relationship now that they were going into heaven. They wondered if divorce was allowed in heaven?

Finally, after 10 weeks passed, they saw St. Peter walking toward them with his laptop in hand, but he looked very tired and worn out.

"Yep, I'm happy to say, we can arrange for you to get married in Heaven," St. Peter said.

"That's wonderful!" Joe said. "But St. Peter, ah…, while we were waiting, we wondered if our re-marriage didn't work out, could we get divorced in heaven?"

St Peter looked at the extensive line of people waiting to get into heaven and started to get angry. He shook his head and walked around in circles, and then said, "Oh Hell! Are you screwing with me?"

Joe said, "No... Why are you so angry?"

St. Peter opened his laptop and pounded away at the keys checking on some things. But as he checked he gradually got angrier and angrier.

Trying to control his anger, St. Peter kept muttering to himself, "You two are screwing with me, aren't you? Yes, you are screwing with me..."

"No way," said Joe.

St Peter slammed his laptop down on top of a cloud and said, "It took me 10 weeks to find a Catholic Priest up here. Do you two have any idea how long it's going to take me to find a lawyer! You two aren't ready for heaven yet, go back to earth and have a good life!"

OfferUp [162] and eBay [163]

eBay has been around for years, but we first want to mention OfferUp [164] as this app has you sell your used items instead of throwing useful items in the rubbish. You can download the OfferUp app for free on Google Play or the Apple store.

OfferUp is simple. You take a photo of the item with your smartphone, create a concise description, and sell it using your smartphone.

OfferUp has ratings for buyers and sellers so you can see who has the good ratings and reliability. You can also chat with potential buyers using OfferUp's messaging in the app, and not have to give out your personal info.

eBay is an opportunity to buy products at low prices and sell them at higher prices.

Once you create your free eBay account, you can begin buying and selling on eBay. You track auctions and bids with your smartphone.

Study what eBay currently charges for its commission which is usually 10% from each sale you make which they deduct from the sale proceeds. For beginners, it's best to choose this commission option since you don't pay anything unless you make a sale.

There are other options for monthly fees and after becoming experienced on eBay, decide what is right for you.

eBay allows the use of PayPal for transactions and most transactions on eBay are done through PayPal.

You can rid your home of useful items you no longer use on eBay as you do on OfferUp.

Look up related items on eBay and see what they are selling for on eBay and review your competition and whether the items are attracting bids? Search eBay's "Completed Listings" in the "Advanced Search Options" to see what comparable items actually sold for.

There is a way on eBay to tell you what items sold for. You click on "Advanced Search" link, next to the search box at the top of eBay pages.

Then enter two or three words that describe the item in the keyword field. After you enter the keywords, select the "Completed listings" option and click the search button and you will see results of what items sold for.

If you want to know what items sell the most on eBay check out CrazyLister [165] to see what the top-selling items are. Keep in mind you can purchase related items if you can acquire them at a lower cost and then upsell them on eBay.

Start small (and learn how it all works) and work your way up to upselling more expensive items on your way to actively earning income on eBay as a lot of people find this worthwhile.

You need to keep your customers happy to keep your feedback excellent since black marks against you will hurt future sales. You should respond right away to all inquiries in a friendly manner and try to help the customer the best you can.

Don't misrepresent or exaggerate what you are selling. If you are selling a damaged item, describe the damage clearly and make that known to the buyer to avoid bad feedback and/or refunds.

You sell on eBay by auction or at a fixed price. The auctions method requires you to set a starting price and whether the auction will be 3 to 10 days. A longer auction allows buyers more time to bid.

You can choose a "Buy it Now" option but pick a price you're comfortable with after researching what similar items have sold for on eBay.

Shopify [166]

Shopify will help you set up your own online store to sell your own products. Shopify supplies you with a web domain, hosting, payments, etc.

The cost of running a Shopify store varies depending on the program you choose. Fees begin at $29 per month and about 3% in fees from every sale you make. Shopify offers a 14-day free trial if you are new to Shopify.

Shopify has most everything you need to set up your store. Once you have your website up and running, you are responsible for directing traffic to your site. Shopify suggests 6 practical ways [167] to build traffic to your site:

- o Send free samples of your products to Instagram Influencers who have hundreds of thousands of followers.

- o Reach out to well-known bloggers, vloggers, and the press.

- o Use Redditt to publicize your store.

- o Get your friends and family to share your new store with everyone they know.

o Engage people on Twitter.

o Write an article or a long testimonial featuring and complimenting Influencers with large audiences and send it to them for publication on their site.

Over the years, Shopify has been highly successful in helping people set up online stores and giving assistance in most aspects of an online store.

As you become more known and get more visitors, your sales will correspondingly increase. It takes ongoing effort and time for success, and it becomes easier as you get more successful.

As more people begin to visit your Shopify site, your sales will begin to increase over time. You will be earning income and Shopify tries to have all the information you need to become successful on its site. You don't have to search a lot of other sources for information.

Since Shopify earns more money when you earn more money, Shopify wants you to succeed and wants to help you have a successful store.

Big Cartel [168]

If you are looking for another site that helps you set up an online store, try Big Cartel which competes with Shopify in the online store area. Big Cartel costs less than Shopify.

Aliexpress [169] and Everbuying [170]

Dropshipping is a way to earn active income where you don't have to buy and store the products you sell. When you sell something, you buy it from a third party at a lower price and the third-party ships it to your customer.

The downside of dropshipping is that the margins (the profits you make) are low, and there are other problems like availability of the product(s) you are selling, shipping the items, rising shipping costs, customer service, etc. You must keep your customers happy, and if they receive damaged goods or goods that arrive late, they may not use you again.

In other words, Dropshipping is a process where you don't buy products and hold them in storage yourself until you sell them. Instead, you find the product you wish to sell in countries that sell at a low cost such as China or India.

When someone buys the product from you (at a high price), you arrange with the site from where you are buying the product (at a low price) and have them ship the product you are selling to your buyer.

Some people who practice Dropshipping locate products at a low cost on Aliexpress or Everbuying (for example), and then promote the product in their blog or in a comprehensive (BETUM) review article.

You could also earn commissions by becoming an Aliexpress Affiliate or an Everbuying Affiliate, but you receive a set commission rather than being able to set your own margin.

Here is an example of dropshipping:

Assume you like to sell magic tricks. You've written an article on how great the trick(s) is and you post the article on a high traffic magic trick site.

You do not have to buy hundreds of the magic tricks you've written about in your review and then hold them in storage. Instead, when someone orders the new magic trick from you, you purchase the trick from say a Chinese wholesaler like Everbuying and have it shipped to your buyer.

You act as the middleman in these transactions and customers place their order through you. So, it's best to choose products which you can sell for a very high margin to cover your costs. Also, try to choose small products of high quality to avoid high storage costs, shipping costs, and returns.

If a customer places an order with you and pays the cost of the item into your bank account, the customer needs to get an automated receipt and confirmation telling when he can expect to receive the item.

You then place your order with say, Everbuying and pay for it and have it shipped to your buyer. You pay a lower cost for the item and shipping and handling charges. You then receive an email telling you when it will be shipped to your buyer and a tracking number.

If everything goes fine, you make a profit on the margin between your cost of the item and shipping and handling charges, and how much the buyer paid you for the magic trick.

149

There are obstacles. You may find an item you want to sell but the source won't allow you to buy just one item at a time. So, you must either find another source or take your chances buying a hundred or more of the magic tricks.

Make sure you plan correctly and try hard not to buy more than you can sell. Have the right plan along with the right marketing, etc., in place before you spend your own money.

*

Joe's wife was on a business trip at a convention in Las Vegas that was poorly attended so she came home late at night one day early.

She quietly put her bags down and tiptoed up the stairs and quietly opened the door to the bedroom.

As the door opened wider, the dim light from the hallway illuminated the bed and she was shocked to see 4 legs under the covers instead of two!

She reached for a 5-iron in the corner of the bedroom and repeatedly slammed it into the bodies under the blanket as hard as she could.

Exhausted, she staggered down the stairs and went into the den to have a drink. As she entered the den, she saw her husband, Joe, sitting down reading a book.

"Hi sweetheart!" Joe said. "Your parents have come to visit. They're using our bedroom. It's still early. Go up and say hello to them."

Instagram [171]

You can sell your products on Instagram and generate income advertising for products in your niche. Ad revenue comes from companies, businesses, advertisers, etc. that want to use your Instagram account to advertise products to your followers. The more quality followers you have, the greater the chance that product advertisers will contact you.

You set up your Instagram account with a theme matching your niche and choose a suitable user name.

It's great if you have a logo as you should use the same logo, bio, and name (if available) on all your social media accounts, as well as in everything you do online for consistency. Consistency helps build your brand.

Also, when setting up your account, be sure to fully fill in your bio information and include your website if you have one.

You should try to stay within your theme since if you change your theme and have pictures of different subjects, you risk losing followers.

Your focus is to build as many followers who are genuinely interested in your theme and love your pictures, videos, and products. Use only the best photos and videos and don't lower the quality and artisanship you put into your Instagram account.

Use hashtags. Like photos and videos of other Instagrammers in your niche as people appreciate your interest and will follow you back if you have a theme they like.

Keep your posts entertaining and educational to your followers (BETUM posts). Try to post at least 2 times a day (once in the morning before work starts and once in the evening after work finishes). Don't over post as it may make you look like you are begging.

Use the app, Crowdfire,[172] if you like it. It will tell you when the best times to post when most people are on social media.

If you find there is a great interest in a certain product in your niche, tell the manufacturers marketing department about it as they might consider you in the future as someone they could advertise on and compensate you.

It takes time to develop a successful Instagram account so be patient in your efforts as it may be well worth it overall.

Amazon Mechanical Turk [173]

Amazon Mechanical Turk is extremely low pay but gives you something to do – a starter. Amazon Mechanical Turk or "Mturk" is a crowdsourcing site which recruits people (known as Providers, or "Turkers") and helps businesses (known as Requesters) to coordinate human intelligence to solve problems that computers are not able to solve. Turkers do "human intelligence tasks" known as HITs. Amazon describes it as jobs that require human intelligence.

Because of the low pay, we weren't sure if we should mention this site in this book, but on the other hand, as your online endeavors grow you may find the need to crowdsource many people to perform a task a computer isn't able to do like picking the right book cover, perform market research, etc. That is, you might use this site as a "Requester" in the future to help you with your online businesses.

Businesses submit tasks like: 1) choosing the best color or photograph, 2) whether people actually understand written instructions as they are written, and if not, then the Business knows it has to rewrite those instructions, 3) reviewing images and judging which picture best represent a product, etc.

Other jobs Turkers do are:

- o Classifying objects in satellite imagery.

- o Deleting duplicate or editing business listings that are incomplete.

- Verifying restaurant or other business details such as phone numbers and hours of operation.

- Turkers ask questions from a computer or mobile device about a topic and return the results.

- Understand and answer market research questions and survey taking.

- Find specific things in large legal and government documents.

- And much more.

Providers or "Turkers" browse the many tasks listed and chose which ones to perform and get paid for completing the task.

In the past, businesses had to hire many people to perform these HITs, but Amazon Mechanical Turk makes it a lot less expensive for businesses to get results and Turkers are available in 30 countries 24x7.

Most tasks don't need a lot of work, and the pay is minimal. If you're looking for something to do at home with extraordinarily little pay, read further on the site of Amazon Turk. [174]

Fulfillment By Amazon (FBA) [175]

Amazon "FBA" means Fulfillment by Amazon, and this is a popular way to earn online income. Amazon FBA sells your products for you. Once you set up a product for sale, you derive passive income as Amazon handles most of the work for you including the all-important customer service. You must give Amazon FBA a lot of ongoing attention when choosing products to sell to be successful. You need time to find the right products, research the saleability of the product, and the reviews of the product, etc.

Ideally, if you are lucky enough to buy great products at exceptionally low prices (such as a clearance or going out of business sale), you ship them to Amazon to store and sell for you. Be sure the items are quality items without damage.

Remember Amazon wants you to be successful and if you make money with a lot of sales, Amazon makes money as well. So, they will help you the best they can.

To begin FBA, the first step is to set up an account with Amazon Seller Central. When you set up an FBA Account through Amazon Seller Central, you have the choice of a "Personal Account" versus a "Professional Account" (about $40 per month fee to Amazon).

A Personal FBA Account allows you to sell up to 40 items per month only paying charges to Amazon when your items sell. If products are large and heavy they will be expensive to store and ship.

Once you set up your FBA account, you will find Amazon offers you a Fulfillment by Amazon Revenue Calculator, so you can determine an estimate of the Amazon storage and shipping fees.

The second step of Amazon FBA is after you set up your account, you ship your products to Amazon. Amazon stores your products in the Amazon fulfillment center. They also process all the purchases, ship the products to purchasers, and do the all-important and excellent Amazon customer service by following up with the purchaser over any issues.

Finding the right products to sell can be difficult and time-consuming. Use price comparison sites on the net to help you figure out whether you can make money when reselling on Amazon FBA. There are many price comparison sites and select one you are comfortable with. To find these sites, just google price comparison sites. You will see sites like NexTag,[176] PriceGrabber,[177] Shopzilla,[178] and many more.

Search for products you are passionate about making sure comparable products are selling well on Amazon.

You can figure out if a product is selling well if the product has many excellent reviews. The hardest part is to buy products to sell which are at least 40-45% (or more) cheaper than what similar products are selling for on Amazon. You want to create as wide a margin as possible since you'll have to pay storage, shipping and packaging charges. The more margin you have the better, of course.

Since you will be paying for storage and shipping and handling, the ideal product would be small, so you won't have to pay large storage fees.

Use Amazon Marketing Services to advertise your products on Amazon since that's where millions are shopping.

Wish.com [179]

Check out Wish.com which offers a similar FBA program like Amazon.

Upwork [180]

Upwork is an exceptionally large site where you can offer your skills to the millions of people looking for skilled people to complete projects. There is a lot of competition on UpWork because of the many people that use it.

You can join for free and check out ongoing jobs or projects by category and apply for the jobs or projects you prefer.

If you have any of these skills, consider joining Upwork to sell your skills to an exceptionally large market of people. Upwork looks for skills in these categories:

- All Web, Mobile & Software Dev
- Desktop Software Development
- eCommerce Development
- Game Development
- Mobile Development
- Product Management
- QA & Testing
- Scripts & Utilities
- Web Development
- Web & Mobile Design
- Other - Software Development
- IT & Networking
- All IT & Networking
- Database Administration
- ERP / CRM Software
- Information Security
- Network & System Administration
- Other - IT & Networking
- Data Science & Analytics
- All Data Science & Analytics
- A/B Testing
- Data Visualization
- Data Extraction / ETL
- Data Mining & Management
- Machine Learning

- Quantitative Analysis
- Other - Data Science & Analytics
- Engineering & Architecture
- All Engineering & Architecture
- 3D Modeling & CAD
- Architecture
- Chemical Engineering
- Civil & Structural Engineering
- Contract Manufacturing
- Electrical Engineering
- Interior Design
- Mechanical Engineering
- Product Design
- Other - Engineering & Architecture
- Design & Creative
- All Design & Creative
- Animation
- Audio Production
- Graphic Design
- Illustration
- Logo Design & Branding
- Photography
- Presentations
- Video Production
- Voice Talent
- Other - Design & Creative
- Writing
- All Writing

- o Academic Writing & Research
- o Article & Blog Writing
- o Copywriting
- o Creative Writing
- o Editing & Proofreading
- o Grant Writing
- o Resumes & Cover Letters
- o Technical Writing
- o Web Content
- o Other - Writing
- o Translation
- o All Translation
- o General Translation
- o Legal Translation
- o Medical Translation
- o Technical Translation
- o Legal
- o All Legal
- o Contract Law
- o Corporate Law
- o Criminal Law
- o Family Law
- o Intellectual Property Law
- o Paralegal Services
- o Other - Legal
- o Admin Support
- o All Admin Support
- o Data Entry

- Personal / Virtual Assistant
- Project Management
- Transcription
- Web Research
- Other - Admin Support
- Customer Service
- All Customer Service
- Customer Service
- Technical Support
- Other - Customer Service
- Sales & Marketing
- All Sales & Marketing
- Display Advertising
- Email & Marketing Automation
- Lead Generation
- Market & Customer Research
- Marketing Strategy
- Public Relations
- SEM - Search Engine Marketing
- SEO - Search Engine Optimization
- SMM - Social Media Marketing
- Telemarketing & Telesales
- Other - Sales & Marketing
- Accounting & Consulting
- All Accounting & Consulting
- Accounting
- Financial Planning
- Human Resources

o   Management Consulting

Set up a profile of your skills and your experience. Review what your future competitors offer in skills and what they charge.

If you don't have much experience, make low offers on jobs to get the experience and add the experience to your CV. The more experience you have, the more you will stand out.

When you complete a job, ask the client for a testimonial so you can add the testimonials to your CV to promote yourself further.

*

A man decided to have a complete physical examination at a well-known clinic to get himself completely checked out.

After two days of tests, he met with the physician in charge who told him he was doing "fine" for his age.

Concerned about what "fine" meant, he asked the doctor, "Do you think I'll live to reach 85?"

The doctor replied, "Do you smoke cigarettes or fine cigars?

"Nope." Said the man.

"Do you drink fine wines, excellent brandies, or any kind of alcohol?"

"No, I don't." The man replied.

"Do you eat filet mignon steaks, fried chicken, bacon and cheese omelets, or barbequed ribs?"

"No, I avoid those foods." The man replied.

"Do you spend time in the sunshine, playing golf, or at the beach, or boating?"

"No, I don't," the man replied.

"Do you chase women, go to casinos, or the horse track?"

"No, I don't do any of that, hell, I haven't ever done any of that." The man said.

The doctor studied his charts, then looked at the man and said, "Then why do you give a sh#t if you live to be 85?"

Zazzle [181]

Zazzle has three aspects to it for designers, manufacturers and affiliate marketers. The Designers produce original designs and put them on products manufactured by others. Affiliate marketers sell the products for commissions.

People who shop on Zazzle are shopping for something unique like clothing on this e-retailer known as Zazzle.

There are 3 ways to make money on Zazzle:

1. For Designers, you create your products (e.g. wedding invitation designs, clothing, T-Shirts, etc.) and work with independent manufacturers of products you are going to enhance with your design.

Under the "Zazzle Designer Program," Designers open a free account and set up a Zazzle store. It is up to the designer to market and promote the products he designs. You will need traffic so apply the methods in this book on how to increase traffic to your Zazzle site.

Your traffic will increase over time if you continually make innovative designs and apply them to various products. For example, some designers upload one design a day and use the design on 10 assorted products. After a year you'll have created over 3,000 products and that should make you easier to appear on Zazzle searches. The most successful designers on Zazzle have thousands of products.

2. For "Makers," (i.e. manufacturers of products who want to sell their products through the Zazzle platform), you don't have to first ship your products like you do when you use Amazon FBA. A maker sells his product via Zazzle and then shows its products on the Zazzle site. Makers show customers what they can make, and the maker ships the goods directly to the customer.

3. Affiliate marketing: Zazzle offers affiliate marketing of products as well so if you like affiliate marketing, you might want to look at Zazzle's affiliate marketing program [182] and earn commissions.

Etsy [183] and Café Press [184]

Etsy and Café Press are competitive sites like Zazzle for designers to sell custom products.

Soundcloud [185]

Soundcloud is a site for music lovers and artists to market their original work. It is an online audio distribution site based in Germany. There are millions of users who upload the music. Music artists record, promote and share their own original music with Soundcloud users.

Ads are played between the songs and artists are paid money for each advertisement that is played, just as YouTubers are paid for the ads watched by their viewers and ad money goes right to the artists.

The more popular your sound is, the more viewers you will get, and the more you will earn.

You can build a following on Soundcloud by joining groups who enjoy your genre. Use related artist's hashtags to attract attention and help people find your music. #Sinatra, #TaylorSwift, etc.

Craigslist [186]

Check out the Craigslist in your area and review the "Jobs" sections for a variety of work available. Click on "Gigs" as well for specific ads offering money for services. Some people get paid more on Craigslist than they do on Fiverr for the same services.

Cash Back - Ebates [187]

Ebates offers cash back at major stores. Ebates made arrangements with major stores where Ebates is paid a commission for sending you as a customer to their store.

You set up a Cash Back account on Ebates, and if you buy an item at a store Ebates referred you to, Ebates gets a commission from the store, and Ebates shares the commission with you as Cash Back into your Cash Back account on the Ebates app.

You access the cash in your account via PayPal.

Dosh [188]

Dosh is similar Ebates, but you get paid right in the store after you purchase – it is an in-store cashback when you purchase.

Field Agent [189]

Download the Field Agent App on your phone and earn income doing market research. Field Agent explains their site as: "You put the app on your phone and earn money by going into stores using your smartphone to collect photos, video, and information from stores and many other locations… and this information is often used by businesses to better serve customers just like you."

Postmates [190]

You can work as a courier in major US cities. Postmates [191] is an on-demand delivery app where customers who need a courier can find and hire a courier very quickly for picking up items in a restaurant, or groceries, office supplies, etc. and delivering it. Postmates explains their services to customers as, "Anything, anywhere, anytime. We get it."

People interested in being couriers should review the site and sign up "Joining the Fleet."

Amazon Flex [192]

Another opportunity to work as a courier is through Amazon Flex where you deliver Amazon Packages.

Uber Eats [193]

Uber Eats is another opportunity to work as a courier.

VIPKID [194]

If you like to teach there are teaching opportunities online at VIPKID and check out this page which explains how to qualify for VIPKID. [195] There are opportunities to teach English as a second language online.

Webinars

Webinars generate income and increase your traffic. Webinars are videos of content created by you to inform people of your products or service and how they can learn new things or live better, etc., after learning about it from you.

Most webinars are free and last between 30 minutes to an hour. People tend to lose interest in a Webinar if it goes on too long. If it's too short, it tends to look like you a simply pitching what you sell.

You want your Webinar to have BETUM quality, (Again, BETUM means: Beneficial, Entertaining, Thought-provoking, Unique, and a Memorable experience). A BETUM Webinar will make people spread the word about you and help you find new customers while educating present customers.

Try not to sell your attendees anything at first. Outline your plan and spell out your marketing to attract attendees to attend a webinar. At the end of the webinar offer them something of higher value which will be genuinely beneficial to them. This can be something absolutely free at the end of the webinar like a BETUM quality PDF on getting more traffic.

Then at the end of the PDF you give out for free, sell something of even higher value to them in your niche where they will learn more about what the webinar is about. Something that will help them earn income.

It's extremely important to show you have a genuine and sincere intention of helping your clients.

You need to keep their attention throughout the whole webinar. Don't keep preaching to the attendees. It's easier and more interesting to give them true life examples of how your ideas or products really work. Consider giving the attendees homework at the end of the webinar to be discussed at your next webinar.

Here is a detailed analysis of attracting people and giving your information free to them:

- o Initial awareness. Your followers in your niche become aware of the existence of a solution when the webinar begins.

- o Catching their interest. You continue with an exciting opening to keep their attention focused, e.g., an actual case history. Once you deeply catch their interest, discuss research you've done to catch more of their interest.

- o Evaluate your product with your competition's products and simply explain

173

why your product is better. Is it cheaper?
Higher Quality? Better researched?

- Let them freely decide if they want your
  product or not. This takes time for most
  people.

- Let them buy and negotiate if you must.
  Offer bonus information or products to help
  them decide.

- Allow the attendees time to reevaluate
  whether they genuinely want to purchase.
  This shows your sincerity in trying to help
  them and not force them to buy anything.

- After they buy, make yourself available and
  leave yourself open to answer any questions
  they might have to help them. If your
  product produces results for them, they will
  want to purchase other products from you.

Webinars are good for many people who prefer to
learn by listening to what you are offering rather
than reading and studying about it.

Most importantly, you don't want any attendee to go
away from the webinar thinking your webinar was a
waste of time. Give high-value content to attendees

who want to learn more about your niche. You may even want to not sell them anything at all at the webinar. Just provide great content which will lead them to your next webinar where you might begin to sell to them.

If you get really good at Webinars and they are well attended, you might even consider having attendees pay a small amount to attend your next webinar if it has high-quality information, or if you are having a well-known influencer or expert joining you in your webinar.

Once you've written a script for your webinar (see the next sub-section for help in writing your script from Upwork people), GoToWebinar.com [196] as it has been the most used platform for webinars. They will help you with everything, but they charge for their service.

Or, look at AnyMeeting.com [197] which is less expensive.

Upwork help with webinars [198]

If you want help in creating your online webinar, use Upwork [199] or other job sites to find excellent content writers and webinar scriptwriters. Read the reviews about the person you may hire. The good writers are expensive so discuss the project with several until you find the right person.

To stir up interest in your webinar:

- o Use the techniques in the How to Increase Traffic Section Two of this book focusing on your niche to reach people genuinely interested in your subject.

- o Write articles/comments, etc. on high traffic blogs mentioning your webinar.

- o Ask influencers and/or anyone and everyone else you know to mention or post information about your webinar. Tell everyone you will return the favor and mention the influencer's webinars on your site and help everyone else who spread the word for you that you will help promote their project when requested.

- o Post in Facebook Groups, LinkedIn Groups, Google+ Communities, Instagram, Twitter, all focused on your niche.

- o Plan to send reminder emails to those who register for your webinar.

If you create an amazing webinar which creates a great amount of interest, you will get more attendees for your next webinar.

If your webinar becomes very popular you can list the webinar on Clickbank as a product and have the thousands of affiliates on Clickbank sell it for you.

Or, you could put your webinar on your YouTube Channel, but you would need millions of views to create a substantial income from YouTube ad revenue. In the very least, posting on YouTube gives you added exposure.

If you don't have your own product, but you discover a product that has "BETUM" quality, do a webinar on the product and earn a commission on the sale of the product through Affiliate Marketing.

For example, if you are selling information on how to hit a faster Tennis First Serve or a faster Second Serve, create a webinar demonstrating the techniques and mention toward the end of the seminar you offer a more comprehensive Tennis Instructional Guide on many other Tennis techniques.

Remember you can make your Tennis Instructional Guide available on Amazon as an eBook, on Clickbank, on your YouTube Channel, on your tennis groups on Facebook and tennis communities on Google+, Reddit, Craigslist, etc. Use #tennisserve, #tennis or any other hashtags for keywords relevant to your Tennis Guide.

Finally, be sincere. It's important to keep an intention of helping people throughout your webinar rather than trying to persuade them to spend money. Showing a sincere desire to help others is a refreshing attitude over the overused sell, sell, sell, call to action, etc. which inundates the web.

Guru.com [200]

Guru.com is another site like UpWork where people hire your services. Guru.com has over 3,000,000 members, and it's a new site. You get paid for completing milestones on a project.

*

Two old retired lawyers went golfing and both severely sliced their drives. They were deep in the rough searching for their errant tee shots. Neither of them wanted to lose a new ball so they searched and searched and eventually wandered off the golf course and came upon a pair of tracks.

They stopped and examined the tracks closely. The first old lawyer announced, "My ball hit these tracks and probably rolled down this way somewhere and I'm going to follow these tracks."

The second old lawyer responded, "Our golf balls couldn't possibly go that way down these tracks – at least not extremely far. I'm not going to waste my time or this golf round searching for your ball in that direction. Besides any idiot could easily see by looking at the level of the land, our balls probably went the opposite way!"

Each old attorney believed himself to have the superior analysis of the situation, and they both bitterly argued on and on. Neither of them would back off from their argument, and they were still arguing heavily when the train hit them.

Fiverr [201]

You can sell your skills on Fiverr - a high traffic site.

Fiverr has a vast array of skill services offered for sale to the public. Here is a general list of the many types of skills offered on Fiverr and take a close look at the examples of skills available on Fiverr. Register and set up a page with Fiverr to offer your skills:

In the Graphic and Design area, people offer their skills for:

- o Logo Design
- o Business Cards & Stationery
- o Illustration
- o Cartoons & Caricatures
- o Flyers & Brochures
- o Book & Album Covers
- o Packaging Design
- o Web & Mobile Design
- o Social Media Design
- o Banner Ads

- Photoshop Editing
- 3D & 2D Models
- T-Shirts & Merchandise
- Presentation Design
- Infographics
- Vector Tracing
- Invitations, and more

In the Digital Design area, people offer their skills for:

- Social Media Marketing
- SEO
- Content Marketing
- Video Marketing
- Email Marketing
- Search & Display Marketing
- Marketing Strategy
- Web Analytics
- Influencer Marketing
- E-Commerce Marketing
- Mobile Advertising
- Music Promotion and more.

In the writing area, people offer skills for:

- Resumes & Cover Letters

- o Proofreading & Editing
- o Translation
- o Creative Writing
- o Business Copywriting
- o Research & Summaries
- o Articles & Blog Posts
- o Press Releases
- o Transcription
- o Legal Writing and more.

In Video and Animation, people offer skills for:

- o Whiteboard & Animated Explainers
- o Intros & Animated Logos
- o Promotional Videos
- o Editing & Post Production
- o Lyric & Music Videos
- o Spokesperson Videos
- o Animated Characters & Modeling
- o Short Video Ads
- o Live Action Explainers, and more.

In the music and audio area, people offer skills for:

- o Voice Over
- o Mixing & Mastering
- o Producers & Composers
- o Singer-Songwriters
- o Session Musicians & Singers

- o Jingles & Drops
- o Sound Effects, and more.

In the programming and tech area, people offer skills for:

- o WordPress
- o Website Builders & CMS
- o Web Programming
- o Ecommerce
- o Mobile Apps & Web
- o Desktop applications
- o Support & IT
- o Chatbots
- o Data Analysis & Reports
- o Databases
- o User Testing, and more.

In the business area, people offer skills for:

- o Virtual Assistant
- o Market Research
- o Business Plans
- o Branding Services
- o Legal Consulting
- o Financial Consulting
- o Business Tips
- o Presentations
- o Career Advice

- o   Flyer Distribution and more.

In the Fun & Lifestyle area, people offer their skills for:

- o   Showing and making products in the Arts and Crafts area
- o   Counselors who offer Relationship Advice
- o   Fitness experts including advice on Health, Nutrition
- o   Astrology Readings
- o   Genealogy searches
- o   How to succeed at Gaming
- o   Makers and designers of Greeting Cards & Videos
- o   Creators of so-called "Viral Videos"
- o   Set up of Pranks and Stunts
- o   Yes, even Celebrity Impersonators for parties etc.

The competition on Fiverr is heavy. Because of the competition and other factors, people offering their skills and services discount their services. When you start out on Fiverr, you offer your services on Fiverr at a competitive rate after you research what your Fiverr competitors are charging.

To get reviews you should discount your services as well. Then spread the word on all your social media, social media groups, email lists, etc. about your Fiverr site and what you charge.

In order to get started on Fiverr, tell people about yourself and your excellent skills. Tell them you will do an excellent job at a much lower price than normal since you are just starting out. Tell them you are only doing it at these prices to get started and to get reviews and testimonials. People like to help and get a bargain at the same time, especially if you can show them samples of your excellent work.

If you find you like selling your services on Fiverr, branch out to offering other types of services to increase your presence on Fiverr. There are sites which offer book editing, book formatting, book covers (everything to help you with an eBook or paperback book).

Check out the Fiverr sites of your potential competitors to see what they charge customers, what the customers get, and how they present their services. Some Fiverr pages have professional videos. Look at the best ones in your niche which Fiverr usually puts up front if they have a lot of high rated reviews.

Most successful people who offer services on Fiverr deliver more than what the customer expects to earn high ratings.

Final Thoughts

There are many exciting opportunities online to earn income. We hope you find one that interests you and we wish you the best in all that you do.

We wanted to end with inspirational and motivational quotes from remarkably successful people and hope you do very well and become successful along with treating your valued customers very well!

"The key to success is to set realistic customer expectations, and then not to just meet them, but to exceed them - preferably in unexpected and helpful ways."

-Richard Branson

"We see our customers as invited guests to a party, and we are the hosts. It's our job every day to make

every important aspect of the customer experience a little bit better."

-Jeff Bezos

"Sell good merchandise at a reasonable profit and treat your customers like human beings, and they will always come back for more."

- Leon Leonwood Bean, aka L. L. Bean

Joe was traveling through the Everglades and stopped at a little bar. He walked in and noticed an old sign hanging by the bar:

IF YOU CAN PASS THE TEST, FREE BEER FOR A YEAR.

Joe scratched his head and asked the proprietor, "Sir, what is... "The Test"?

The proprietor looked at Joe and shook his head. "You really want to know?"

"Yeah, just curious. I like beer especially free beer," Joe replied.

The proprietor says, "Well, here's how it goes. You drink that gallon bottle of Prairie Fire."

"What's Prairie Fire?" Joe asked.

"Tabasco Sauce and Vodka. You got to drink the whole thing down all at once – no stoppin' and you can't grimace one bit. Next, there's a gator back there with a sore tooth - the proprietor points out the window. You gotta pull that tooth out with your bare hands. Third, there's a lady upstairs getting on in her years and she's never had a climax. You gotta make things right for her – you know what I'm talking about?"

Joe sits there shaking his head. "As much as I'd like free beer, that's crazy. You know I've done some crazy things but that's ridiculous."

Well, Joe drinks a few, then sits up and says, "Wherez that Plareeee Phire?" Then Joe grabs the gallon jug and chugs it all down. His face is redder than the rising sun, tears are streaming down his face. He slams the empty gallon bottle down on the bar and staggers out back.

The others at the bar hear hair-raising grunts and loud roars. They look out the window at the pen outside and see the huge alligator struggling to get away while Joe is dragging it back into the pen. There's more even louder roaring and grunting. Then eerie silence.

Joe staggers out of the pen. His shirt and pants are ripped to shreds and he's bleeding from scratches and cuts all over his body as he staggers back into the bar.

"Okay," Joe says, "Where's that lady with the sore tooth?"

We Hope You Found This Book Helpful!

Thank you for reading this book.

We hope you enjoyed this book and use it as a reference.

If you liked this book, we would appreciate your giving us a brief review on Amazon or Goodreads.

Our friend Joe and his funny exploits will be back in our next online income book!

Thank you very much.

Bruce Miller and The TeamGolfwell

We Want to Hear From You

Thomas Edison, image from Creative Commons

"Opportunity is missed by most people because it is dressed in overalls and looks like work."

- Thomas Edison

The internet is constantly changing. New sites and new ways of earning passive income, active income and increasing your traffic arise every day.

We will be writing more on this subject as more changes occur over time. If you want a notification of when our next book covering online income and

191

increasing your traffic comes out, please email us at TeamGolfwell@gmail.com.

Thank you very much.

Sincerely,

Bruce Miller and TeamGolfwell

P.S. We love to hear the thoughts and suggestions of our readers on anything and please contact us at TeamGolfwell@gmail.com.

www.TeamGolfwell.com

Team Golfwell's Other Books

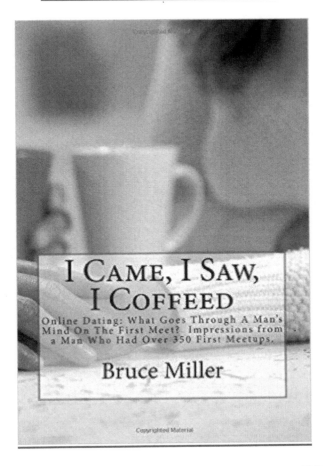

I Came, I Saw, I Coffeed - Online Dating: Why Didn't He Call Me Back? Impressions from a Man Who Had Over 350 First Meetups

Team Golfwell's Other Books

Latecomers to Love: Online Dating for Mature Men and Women: Why Didn't He Call Me Back? Why Didn't She Want a Second Date?

Team Golfwell's Other Books

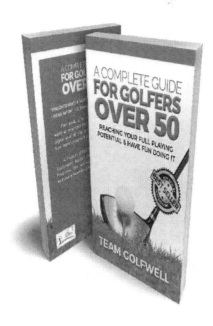

A Complete Guide For Golfers Over 50: Reaching Your Full Playing Potential & Have Fun Doing It. (Over 300 pages)

Team Golfwell's Other Books

Golf FitnessGolf Fitness: An All-Inclusive Golf Fitness Program For Golfers Only

Team Golfwell's Other Books

Absolutely Hilarious Adult Golf Joke Book

Team Golfwell's Other Books

Team Golfwell's Other Books

Fascinating Golf Stories and More Hilarious Adult Golf Jokes (Second in the Golfwell Adult Joke Book Series)

Bruce Miller, B.A. J.D. and Team Golfwell

Team Golfwell's Other Books

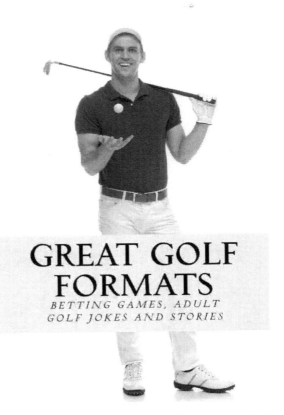

Great Golf Formats: Betting Games, Adult Golf Jokes and Stories

(Third in the Golfwell Adult Joke Book Series)

Team Golfwell's Other Books

Golf Tips and Adult Golf Jokes

(Fourth in Golfwell Adult Joke Book Series)

Team Golfwell's Other Books

Golf Shots: How To Easily Learn a Wide Variety of Shots

Team Golfwell's Other Books

Golf Driving Techniques from Golfing Greats and Golf Stories

Team Golfwell's Other Books

Golf Putting Techniques from Golfing Greats: Proven Putting Techniques from Tiger, Rory, Jason Day, Jordan Spieth, and Others

Team Golfwell's Other Books

Walk the Winning Ways of Golf's Greatests
For Young Golfers, Junior Golfers, First Tee

Team Golfwell's Other Books

What Every Average Golfer Ought to Know:

54 Ways to Lower Your Score That Really Work

Team Golfwell's Other Books

Wonderful Golf Stories: Entertaining Stories from Golfwell's International Story Competition

Team Golfwell's Other Books

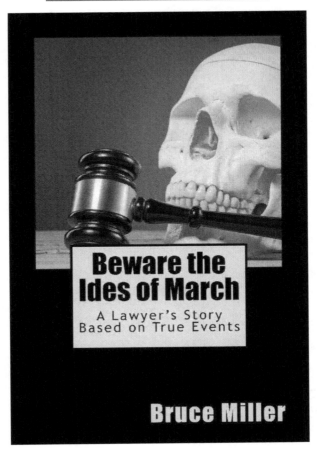

Beware the Ides of March by Bruce Miller a Team Golfwell Member – Based on true events

References

---

[1] Kindle Direct Publishing, https://kdp.amazon.com

[2] CreateSpace, https://www.createspace.com

[3] Content is King Essay by Bill Gates, https://medium.com/@HeathEvans/content-is-king-essay-by-bill-gates-1996-df74552f80d9

[4] Supra.

[5] Supra,

[6] Amazon Marketing Services, supra.

[7] IngramSpark, www.ingramspark.com

[8] Amazon Author Central, https://authorcentral.amazon.com/gp/home

[9] IngramSpark, http://www.ingramspark.com/

[10] BookBub Partners, https://partners.bookbub.com/

[11] Kindleprenuer, https://kindlepreneur.com/

[12] Kobo, https://www.kobo.com/

[13] Apple iBook, https://support.apple.com/en-us/HT201183

[14] Lincoln Cole.net, "Print on Demand: CreateSpace, KDP Print, IngramSpark - Which One Should You Use to Publish Your Book?", https://www.lincolncole.net/tools/print-on-demand-createspace-kdp-print-ingramspark-and-more

[15] ACX, http://www.acx.com

---

[16] "Selling Your Apps Internationally on Amazon", https://developer.amazon.com/blogs/post/Tx2SR9SL9ZHYHU M/Selling-Your-Apps-Internationally-on-Amazon.html

[17] Lending Club, https://www.lendingclub.com

[18] Ibid.

[19] The Lending Club, How it Works, https://www.lendingclub.com/investing/alternative-assets/how-it-works

[20] Fundrise, https://fundrise.com/

[21] Fundrise FAQ, https://fundrise.com/education/faq#item552

[22] Getty Images, https://www.gettyimages.com/

[23] iStockPhotos, https://www.istockphoto.com/

[24] Foap, https://www.foap.com/

[25] Shutterstock, https://submit.shutterstock.com/

[26] Foap Missions, https://www.foap.com/missions

[27] Ibid.

[28] Snapwire, https://www.snapwi.re/photographer

[29] Tony Northrup, https://www.amazon.com/Tony-Northrups-DSLR-Book-Photography-ebook/dp/B006KY2VZ2

[30] AppyPie, https://www.appypie.com/

[31] AppMakr, https://www.appmakr.com/

[32] Upwork, https://www.upwork.com

33 Fiverr, https://www.fiverr.com

34 Amazon App Store, "Marketing Your App," https://developer.amazon.com/marketing-your-app

35 Udemy, https://www.udemy.com

36 Vimeo, https://vimeo.com

37 Skillshare, https://www.skillshare.com

38 Airbnb, https://www.airbnb.com

39 RV Share, https://rvshare.com/

40 Ibid.

41 Acorns, https://www.acorns.com/

42 Ibid.

43 Betterment, https://www.betterment.com/

44 Flippa, https://flippa.com/websites

45 Ibid.

46 AdSense, https://www.google.com/adsense/start

47 YouTube, https://www.youtube.com/

48 Webopedia, https://www.webopedia.com/TERM/S/SEO.html

49 Fiverr, https://www.fiverr.com/

50 Konker, http://www.konker.io/

[51] OzzieUK, https://www.fiverr.com/ozzieuk/create-a-full-seo-campaign-for-your-website

[52] Google Keyword Tool, https://keywordtool.io/

[53] Wordstream KeyWord Tool, https://www.wordstream.com/keywords

[54] https://support.google.com/analytics#topic=3544906

[55] Google Search Console, https://www.google.com/webmasters/tools/home?hl=en

[56] Bing Webmaster Tools, https://www.bing.com/toolbox/webmaster

[57] Google Analytics, https://www.google.com/analytics/

[58] Keyword Tool io, Google, https://keywordtool.io/google

[59] Google Keyword Planner, https://adwords.google.com/home/tools/keyword-planner/

[60] Google Mobile Friendly Test, https://search.google.com/test/mobile-friendly

[61] Dr. Link Check, https://www.drlinkcheck.com/

[62] Google Page Speed, https://developers.google.com/speed/pagespeed/insights

[63] Moz.com open site explorer, https://moz.com/researchtools/ose/

[64] supra.

[65] BuzzBundle, https://www.buzzbundle.com/

[66] BuzzBundle pricing, https://www.buzzbundle.com/order.html

[67] Wikihow, https://www.wikihow.com/Make-a-Unique-Username

[68] Facebook, https://www.facebook.com

[69] Federal Trade Commission, "The FTC Endorsement Guide: What People are Asking," https://www.ftc.gov/tips-advice/business-center/guidance/ftcs-endorsement-guides-what-people-are-asking

[70] Chatfuel, https://chatfuel.com/

[71] Botkit, https://botkit.ai/

[72] Amazon Author Central, "Publishing and Selling on Amazon," https://authorcentral.amazon.com/gp/help/ref=AC_CU_Books-notavail-oop-dyk?topicID=200650270

[73] BookBub, https://www.bookbub.com/partners/pricing

[74] ManyBooks, http://manybooks.net/promote

[75] Get Free eBooks, https://www.getfreeebooks.com/submit-your-ebooks/

[76] Ereader News Today, https://ereadernewstoday.com/bargain-and-free-book-submissions/

[77] ReadCheaply, http://readcheaply.com/

[78] LinkedIn Help, Finding and Joining LinkedIn Groups, https://www.linkedin.com/help/linkedin/answer/186/finding-and-joining-a-linkedin-group?lang=en

[79] TeamGolfwell, "What Would You Do To Convince Someone To Buy Your Services Through the Phone In a Funny Way," https://www.quora.com/What-would-you-do-to-convince-someone-to-buy-your-services-through-the-phone-in-a-funny-way/answer/Bruce-Miller-128

[80] LinkedIn Help, "Who's Viewed Your Profile," https://www.linkedin.com/help/linkedin/answer/42

[81] LinkedIn Help, "Adding a Website to Your Profile," https://www.linkedin.com/help/linkedin/answer/3236/adding-a-website-to-your-profile?lang=en

[82] Google + Communities, https://plus.google.com/communities

[83] Instagram, https://www.instagram.com/

[84] Forbes Article by Brian Rashid, https://www.forbes.com/sites/brianrashid/2017/06/10/15-top-instagram-influencers-you-should-follow/#359703fc6001

[85] Instagram Help Center. "How do I use hashtags?" https://help.instagram.com/351460621611097

[86] Peter Haraway, "The Absolute Beginner's Guide to Taking Great Photographs," https://www.amazon.com/Absolute-Beginners-Guide-Taking-Photographs-ebook/dp/B072MPS3GM

[87] Pinterest, https://www.pinterest.com

[88] HARO, https://www.helpareporter.com/

[89] Quora, https://www.quora.com/

[90] Ibid.

[91] StackExchange, https://stackexchange.com

[92] Redditt, https://www.reddit.com

[93] Facebook Ads, https://web.facebook.com/business/products/ads

[94] Twitter Ads, https://ads.twitter.com/

[95] LinkedIn Ads, https://business.linkedin.com/marketing-solutions/ads

[96] AdWords, https://www.google.co.nz/adwords/express/

[97] Bing Ads, https://secure.bingads.microsoft.com/

[98] Amazon Marketing Services, https://advertising.amazon.com/

[99] Amazon FBA, https://services.amazon.com/fulfillment-by-amazon/benefits.html

[100] Amazon Marketing Services, supra.

[101] Kindle Select, https://kdp.amazon.com/en_US/select

[102] Ibid.

[103] MailChimp, www.mailchimp.com

[104] Mail Chimp, "About the General Data Protection Regulation," https://kb.mailchimp.com/accounts/management/about-the-general-data-protection-regulation

[105] Qzzr, www.qzzr.com

[106] You Tube, https://www.youtube.com/

[107] Fitness Blender, https://www.fitnessblender.com/

[108] Google AdSense, https://www.google.com/adsense/start/

[109] FTC FAQ. "The FTC's Endorsement Guides: What People Are Asking," https://www.ftc.gov/tips-advice/business-center/guidance/ftcs-endorsement-guides-what-people-are-asking

[110] Clickbank, https://www.clickbank.com/

[111] Amazon Associates, https://affiliate-program.amazon.com/

[112] eBay Partner Program, https://partnernetwork.ebay.com/

[113] Walmart, https://affiliates.walmart.com/linksharesignupnew

[114] AliExpress.com, https://portals.aliexpress.com/

[115] ShareASale, https://www.shareasale.com/

[116] CJ Affiliate, http://www.cj.com/

[117] DigiResults, https://www.digiresults.com/

[118] FTC, https://www.ftc.gov/tips-advice/business-center/guidance/ftcs-endorsement-guides-what-people-are-asking

[119] Insta Econ Express, https://www.wpmarketertools.com/insta-ecom-express/

[120] Clickbank, https://www.clickbank.com

[121] Clickbank Support, https://support.clickbank.com/hc/en-us/articles/220364027-Creating-Your-First-Product

[122] Supra. https://affiliate-program.amazon.com/home

[123] Ibid.

124 WordPress, https://wordpress.com

125 GoDaddy, https://wordpress.com

126 eBay Partner Network, https://partnernetwork.ebay.com/

127 eBay Video on Partner Network,
https://partnernetwork.ebay.com/epn-blog/2016/10/affiliate-marketing-101-video-make-money-online/

128 Walmart Affiliate,
https://affiliates.walmart.com/linksharesignupnew

129 Aliexpress, https://portals.aliexpress.com/

130 ShareaSale, https://www.shareasale.com/

131 CJ Affiliate, http://www.cj.com/

132 DigiResults, https://www.digiresults.com/

133 Everbuying, http://www.everbuying.net/affiliate.html

134 AdSense, https://www.google.com/adsense/start

135 Google, AdSense Help,
https://support.google.com/adsense/answer/1346295?hl=en

136 Media.net, https://www.media.net/

137 Google Analytics, https://analytics.google.com/

138 Infolinks, www.infolinks.com/

139 Hubpages, https://hubpages.com

140 HubPages FAQ, https://hubpages.com/faq

141 InfoBarrel, http://www.infobarrel.com/

142 Medium, https://medium.com/creators

143 Swagbucks, https://swagbucks.com

144 Swagbucks, https://www.swagbucks.com/

145 Crowdology, https://crowdology.com/

146 MySurvey, www.mysurvery.com

147 EasyShift, http://www.easyshiftapp.com/

148 EasyShiftApp, www.easyshiftapp.com/

149 FlexJobs, https://www.flexjobs.com/

150 FlexJobs, Brie Weiler Reynolds, "10 Job Categories on the Rise," https://www.flexjobs.com/blog/post/flexible-job-categories-rise/

151 CheckPoint, https://www.checkpoints.com/

152 Checkpoints, https://techcrunch.com/2010/09/27/checkpoints/

153 FieldAgent, https://app.fieldagent.net/

154 Gigwalk, https://gigwalk.com/

155 Gigwalkers, http://www.gigwalk.com/gigwalkers/

156 WorkLLama, https://workllama.com/

157 WorkLLama, "What We Do," https://workllama.com/what-we-do-job-seekers/

158 Taskrabbit, https://www.taskrabbit.com/

[159] DogVacay, https://www.ebay.com

[160] Mobee, https://mobeeapp.com/

[161] AppTrailers, http://www.apptrailers.com/

[162] OfferUp, https://www.OfferUp.com

[163] eBay, https://www.ebay.com

[164] Supra.

[165] CrazyLister, https://crazylister.com/blog/top-selling-items-on-ebay/

[166] Shopify, https://www.shopify.com/

[167] Shopify, "6 Practical and Proven Ways to Drive Traffic to Your New Online Store," https://www.shopify.co.nz/blog/13869029-6-practical-and-proven-ways-to-drive-traffic-to-your-new-online-store

[168] BigCartel, https://www.bigcartel.com/

[169] Aliexpress, https://aliexpress.com

[170] Everbuying, http://www.everbuying.net/

[171] Instagram, http://www.apptrailers.com/

[172] Crowdfire, https://www.crowdfireapp.com/

[173] Amazon Mechanical Turk, https://www.mturk.com/

[174] Ibid.

---

175 Fulfillment by Amazon, https://services.amazon.com/fulfillment-by-amazon/benefits.html

176 Nextag, https://www.nextag.com/

177 PriceGrabber, www.pricegrabber.com/

178 Shopzilla, www.shopzilla.com/

179 Wish.com, https://merchant.wish.com/

180 Upwork, https://www.upwork.com

181 Zazzle, https://www.zazzle.com/

182 Zazzle Affiliates, https://www.zazzle.com/sell/affiliates

183 Etsy, https://www.etsy.com

184 Café Press, https://www.cafepress.com

185 Soundcloud, https://soundcloud.com

186 Craigslist, https://www.checkpoints.com/

187 Ebates, https://www.ebates.com

188 Dosh, https://www.dosh.cash

189 FieldAgent, https://app.fieldagent.net/

190 Postmates, https://postmates.com

191 Ibid.

192 Amazon Flex, https://flex.amazon.com/

193 Uber Eats, https://www.ubereats.com/

---

[194] VIPKID, https://t.vipkid.com.cn/

[195] VIPKID Getting Started, https://t.vipkid.com.cn/faq/getting_started

[196] GoToWebinar.com, https://www.gotowebinar.com

[197] Intermedia Anymeeting.com, https://www.anymeeting.com/

[198] Upwork, https://www.upwork.com/

[199] Ibid.

[200] Guru.com, https://www.guru.com/

[201] Fiverr, https://www.fiverr.com/

Baby Clothes For baby toddler
From Newborn to 6 year of age
1. Drive lic   10mb
Seller acount
Baby Pampars

Made in the USA
Columbia, SC
05 June 2020